Sense Poetry

Little Voices

Edited by Jenni Bannister

First published in Great Britain in 2016 by:

Remus House
Coltsfoot Drive
Peterborough
PE2 9BF
Telephone: 01733 890066
Website: www.youngwriters.co.uk

All Rights Reserved
Book Design by Spencer Hart
© Copyright Contributors 2016
SB ISBN 978-1-78624-243-3

Printed and bound in the UK by BookPrintingUK
Website: www.bookprintinguk.com

Foreword

Dear Reader,

Welcome to this book packed full of sights
and smells, sounds and tastes!

Young Writers' Sense Poetry competition was specifically designed for Key Stage 1 children as a fun introduction to poetry and as a way to think about their senses: what the little poets can see, taste, smell, touch and hear in the world around them. From this starting point the poems could be as simple or as elaborate as the writer wanted, using imagination and descriptive language to conjure a complex image of the subject of their writing, rather than concentrating just on what it looks like.

Given the young age of the entrants we have tried to include as many poems as possible. Here at Young Writers we believe that seeing their work in print will inspire a love of reading and writing and give these young poets the confidence to develop their skills in the future. Poetry is a wonderful way to introduce young children to the idea of rhyme and rhythm and helps learning and development of communication, language and literacy skills.

These young poets have used their creative writing abilities, sentence structure skills, thoughtful vocabulary and, most importantly, their imaginations to make their poems come alive. I hope you enjoy reading them as much as we have.

Jenni Bannister

Editorial Manager

Contents

Sophie Isabel Hardy (6) 1
Judah Aldridge (6) 1
Freya Birney (6) 2
Naomi Adio (6) 2
Marlon Dyke-Wells 3
Krish Munshaw (6) 3
Hamish Oliver Sebastian Quigley (7) 4
Lily Grace Pedder (6) 4

All Saints CE (VA) Primary School, Wellingborough

Zane Cooper (6) 5
Laura Kania (7) 5
Olivia Thomas-Ferrer 6

Allithwaite CE Primary School, Grange-Over-Sands

Nicole Alessenko (6) 6
Kurt Cousins (7) 7
Flynn Myatt (7) 7
Eleanor Ruby Horn (7) 8
Alistair George Hunter (6) 8
Harry Spibey (7) 9
Mackenzie Hodgson (6) 9
Lareece Pocklington (6) 10
Poppy Rose Airey (6) 10

Ardnashee School & College, Londonderry

Sam Carlin (8) 11
Daisy Curry (8) 11

Ashford Hill Primary School, Thatcham

Megan Hall (5) 12
Freddie James Lapham (7) 12
Arthur James Buckingham (5) 13
Olivia Cochrane (6) 13
Edward Liddeatt (5) 14
Archie Thomas (6) 14
Ariana Parkinson Gadd (6) 15

Beechwood Primary School, Crewe

Mesha Evans (7) 15
Ellie-May Morris (6) 16
Honey Jack (6) 16
Lauren Sadler (7) 17
Amy Lynne Chloe Rowland (7) 17
Abbie Marie Parsonage (7) 18
Destiny Potts (7) 18
Danikah (6) 19
Adam Strzelczyk (6) 19
Quinn Dodd (7) 20
Whitney Wollaston (6) 20

Beetham CE Primary School, Milnthorpe

Sophie Hunn (6) 21
Lili Robinson (7) 21
Grace Smith (5) 22
Ted McDowell (6) 22
Lily Sophia Christou (7) 23
Emily Weiss (6) 23
Thomas Goncalves (6) 24
Daniel Gardner (7) 24
Maciej Piszko (6) 25
Holly Jenner (7) 25

Blueberry Park Primary School, Liverpool

Demi George (7) 26
Jaden McConnon (6) 26
Chloe Parker (7) 27
Connor Molloy (7) 27
Scott Eyres (7) 28
Marnie Johnson (7) 28
Kieran McMahon (7) 29
Jurek Pyszczak (5) 29
Ian Birnie (5) 30
Maanaswini Sabat (6) 30
Reception Class Miss Owens 31

Lillie Taplin (5)	32
Hayden Cook (7)	32
Keeley Hart (6)	33
Summer Jones (6)	33
Vanesa Libakova (5)	34
Kyle Williams (5)	34
Oscar Sell (7)	35
Phillip Joseph Lynch (7)	35
Neriah Anthony (6)	36
Verity Cook (5)	36
Emily Jayde Tague (6)	37
Scott Courtney Ashworth (6)	37

Broughton Primary School, Cockermouth

Joshua Clark (6)	38
Holly Graham (6)	38
Willow Richardson (6)	39
Sophia Tzelepi-Jones (5)	39
Shay Williams (6)	40
Samantha Hewitt (6)	40
Millie Rose Graham (5)	41
Lexie Hutchinson (5)	41
Kian Michael Tyson (5)	42
Ewan Abraham (6)	42
Charleigh Taylor (6)	43
Alexander Murray (6)	43
Bethany Lauren Bebb (6)	44

Cartmel CE Primary School, Grange-Over-Sands

Catriona Lilian Bell (7)	44
Charlie Crabtree (7)	45
Henry Crabtree (7)	45
Ollie Hunter-Lowe (7)	46
Brooke Coward (5)	46
James Robert Bland (6)	47

Edge Grove School, Watford

Keya Shona Mistry (6)	47
Kyan Peter Bhupendra Mehta (5)	48
Mohammed Ali Reza (6)	48
Dara Olunloyo (6)	49
Fatemah Asaria (5)	50
Archer Francis Kettle (5)	50

Isabella Little (5)	51
Ehije Izzi-Engbeaya (5)	51
Francesca Mackenzie (5)	52
Joel Abraham Jaffe (6)	52
Caitlin O'Keeffe (6)	53
Charlotte Mai Gardiner (6)	53
Evan Nursiah (6)	54
Hugh Padayachy (6)	54
Amber Hilton (5)	55
Kimaya Kapadia (6)	55
Zachary Oladuji (5)	56
Honor	56
Eniola Opaleye (6)	57

Fairfield Primary School, Stockton-On-Tees

Alfie Ayres (6)	57
Alexa Grace Wiley (6)	58
Joseph Watson (7)	58
Alexander Gaskell (7)	59
Thomas Mbabazi (6)	59
Summer Gibb (7)	60
Xenia Rose Parry (6)	60
Oliver David John Fish (6)	61
Ruby Dinsdale (6)	61
Phoebe Carr Armson (6)	62
Olivia Hobbs (7)	62
Lucy Robertson (6)	63
Levi Graham (7)	63
Joseph Hall (6)	64
Harvey Knowles (6)	64
Holly Cotton (6)	65
Finley Moody (6)	65
Evie Pearce (7)	66
Charlie George Clough (6)	66
Daniel O'Keeffe (7)	67
Ayva Wilde (6)	67
Anna Lin (7)	68
Alfie Brown (6)	68
Lucy Banthorpe (7)	69
Zachary Clark (6)	69
Aimee Dixon (7)	70
Alice Osborne (6)	70
Arden Stephens (7)	71
Callum Lane-Tingle (7)	71

Benjamin O'Donnell (7)	72
Grace Nelson (7)	72
Grace Warnock (6)	73
Hayden Kenning (7)	73
Jacob Reed (6)	74
Jacob Edward Riley (7)	74
Joseph White (7)	75
Kallan Joe Robert Mason (7)	75
Joseph Edward Wrigley (6)	76
Kane Warrick (6)	76
Lincoln Miles Benjamin White (6)	77
Katie Rose Morris (7)	77
Lucas Harley Elliott (6)	78
Millie Eve Gibbon (7)	78
Payton Grace Goodhall (7)	79
Ben Rutter (6)	79

Hillcroft Primary School, Caterham

Paige Reed (5)	80
Veenaa Kistnen (6)	80
Kyle Cheeseman (6)	81
Alexz Davis (6)	81
Jessica Drew Grant (6)	82
Daisy Patton (6)	82
Ethan Russell (5)	83
Ben David Hoey (6)	83
Bella Hill (5)	84
Stanley Hopkins (6)	84
Jake Fuller (5)	85
Blaine Paterson (6)	85
Amelia Krawczyk (6)	86
Kacie Anders (6)	86
Samuel Read (5)	87
George Wilson (5)	87

King's House Preparatory School & Nursery, Luton

Aditi Gampa (6)	88
Ava May Rossiter (7)	88
Dara Akinola (6)	89
Barack Nyamboki (7)	89
Aleena Azam (7)	90
Amber-Zahra Abbas (6)	91
Stephanie Oghenemine Ogban (7)	91

Imaan Shahieen Khan (6)	92
Haaris Javaid (7)	92
Joaquim Bangaroo (7)	93
Kristal Dongbakuro (6)	93
Nahum Joshua Alexis Abiaka (7)	94
Maya Brown (7)	94
Sheharyar Butt (6)	95
Ryyan Akhtar (6)	96
Amaana Rahman (6)	96
Taan Sangha (7)	97
Umar Mazhar (6)	97
Adedamola Adeoti (5)	98
Aansh Lohia (5)	98
Aayan Chowdhry (6)	99
Eugene London Jordan (6)	99
Ayesha Raza (6)	100
Juliette Mitrov (6)	100
Kayla Choto (6)	101
Leeya Naik Ehsan (5)	101
Megan Yu (5)	102
Riley Emerton (6)	102
Joy Hayble (7)	103

Our Lady's Catholic Primary School, Stockport

Ethan Igali (5)	103
Brihanna Sandra Estevao Manuel (4)	104
Lexi Cooper-Jones (5)	104
Kyle James Barlow (5)	105
Annalese Wood (5)	105
Owen Tierney (4)	106

Paradise Primary School, Dewsbury

Safa Qasim (7)	106
Sara Hazi (7)	107
Aisha Bodhania (5)	107
Yusuf Dokrat (8)	108
Khadija Abdelkadir (6)	108
Humayra Patel (6)	109
Khadija Ibrahim (7)	109
Eesa Khan (6)	110
Maryam Bint Tariq (8)	110
Aishah Noor Naeem (7)	111

Abdur-Rahman Obeidi (7) 112
Fatima Zahra Patel (8)........................ 112
Habeebah Raja (7) 113
Abu-Bakr Polli (8) 113
Eesha Ismail (7)................................... 114

Petteril Bank Community School, Carlisle

Aidan Kidd (6)...................................... 114

Rosley CE School, Wigton

Reuben Massey (5) 115
Thea Reid (6).. 115
Oscar Massey (7) 116
Jack Turner (5) 116
Rosemary Elizabeth Quinn (5) 117
Kara Eve Thomlinson (7)..................... 117
Daniel Patrick Keane (6)...................... 118
Felix Broadbent (6) 118
Bella Milburn (6) 119
Hope Vernon (5) 119
Finley Graham (6)................................. 120
Sam Donald (7) 120
Isaac Joe Rumney (5) 121
Charlie Robert Jackson (5).................. 121
Lily Mary Richardson (6)...................... 122
Rory Irving (6)....................................... 122
Hannah Emily Kelly (7)......................... 123
Lucy Knott (6) 123

Tarporley CE Primary School, Tarporley

Halle Miller (7) 124
Samuel M Preston (6)........................... 124
Nathan Anderton (7) 125
Leah Cunningham (7)........................... 125
Harry Leftwick (7) 126
Milly Venning (7)................................... 126
Holly Slaughter (7)............................... 127
Rebecca Line (7) 127
George Wood (6) 128
Marcus Kearney (7)............................... 128
Ella Jones (6)... 129
Jared Mills (7) 129
Aidan Hart (7) 130
Helen Riley (6) 130

Jack Farren (6) 131
Luke O'Hara Clarke (7).......................... 131
Rhys Chambers (7) 132
Gemma Randles (6) 132
Isobelle Allan (6).................................... 133

Towerview Primary School, Bangor

Katie Emma Jordan (6)......................... 133

Upton Cross Primary School, Liskeard

Ethan Greenaway (7) 134
Issy Thom (7)... 134
Naomi Bettison (7)................................ 135
Bobby Easton Evans (7)....................... 135
Lauren Hoare (7) 136
Poppy Amelia Carthew-Hall (7) 136
Caine Hosband (7) 137
Holly Stock (7)....................................... 137
Holly Merriner (7).................................. 138

Well Lane Primary School, Birkenhead

Warren Banks (5) 138
Sophia Kaplansoy (5) 139
Leah Sysum (6) 139
Michael Kinealy (7)................................ 140
Max Hibbert (6)...................................... 140
Maddison Amis (6)................................. 141
Caitlyn Louise Wellman (7)................... 141
Lola Makay (7)....................................... 142
Fletcher Hagan (7)................................. 142

The Poems

Sounds Good!

Gravy bubbles,
Swirly pasta wriggling,
Sizzling sausages wiggling,
Hot dogs hiss.

Cheese wobbles,
Chocolate cake wobbles,
Bacon boils,
Apple stands still.

Frying pancakes,
Popcorn pops,
Sizzling sausages.

I'm hungry!

Sophie Isabel Hardy (6)

Fire!

Fire smells like smoke.
Fire looks like flames.
Fire sounds like scrunching paper.
Fire feels soft and hot.
Fire tastes hot and melting.
Fire!

Judah Aldridge (6)

In The Dark, Dark Woods

In the dark, dark woods
I see trees swaying
I hear foxes barking
I taste apples
I touch foxes' tails
I smell fire burning.

Freya Birney (6)

Winter

Winter sounds like golden, noisy bells
ringing in a church.
Winter feels like cold, frosty snow on my clothes.
Winter looks like beautiful snowflakes
soaring through the air.
Winter tastes like hot chocolate and milk with biscuits.
Winter smells like Christmas presents and a huge hug.

Naomi Adio (6)

What Happens In The Night

Raindrops cling to cobwebs to
Escape from the flames and
Heat.
The rushing crushing sound of fire
Is getting higher and higher.
The smoke is rising near the sky.
The sky is full of smoke and fire.

Marlon Dyke-Wells

Tom And Jerry

Jerry was eating a piece of cheese.
Tom saw it and was not pleased,
Tom heard Jerry biting his teeth,
Tom was ready to eat Jerry's meat.
Cheese tasted yummy,
It filled Jerry's tummy.
Tom smelt Jerry and came in, chasing,
Tom pushed Jerry on ice till he was freezing.

Krish Munshaw (6)

Sounds Good!

Dogs whine
Cats purr
Mice squeak
Cows go *moo*
And cows go *ding dong*
Sheep go *baa*
As they herd into a line
Ducks quack
Goats butt trees
Bunnies go *boing boing*
Honey comes from bees
In the countryside.

Hamish Oliver Sebastian Quigley (7)

The Penguin

I can hear the kicking from the penguin's flippers
I can taste the wind from the penguin island
I can smell the penguin life
I can touch a fluffy, cute penguin in its honour
I can see a fluffy, cute penguin in its home.

Lily Grace Pedder (6)

Iron Man

Iron Man has good hearing.
Iron Man is hard.
Iron Man is strong and metal.
Iron Man smells like oil.
Iron Man looks like metal.
Iron Man looks strong and he looks like a giant.
You can hear Iron Man's engine.

Zane Cooper (6)
All Saints CE (VA) Primary School, Wellingborough

Untitled

Mama smells like perfume and flowers.
Mama looks like a beautiful princess.
Mum sounds like she's singing.
Mama feels like a helpful hand.
Mum tastes like a sweet.
My mama is the best.

Laura Kania (7)
All Saints CE (VA) Primary School, Wellingborough

The Tooth Fairy

The tooth fairy looks like a pretty, beautiful flower.
The tooth fairy smells like candy canes.
The tooth fairy tastes like minty toothpaste.

Olivia Thomas-Ferrer
All Saints CE (VA) Primary School, Wellingborough

One Little Cat

When you stroke cats for a long time
They purr for a long time.
You can hear the cat's miaow,
You can touch the cat's fur.
You can see the cats move,
Cats smell weird,
They lick themselves and look weird.

Nicole Alessenko (6)
Allithwaite CE Primary School, Grange-Over-Sands

Bananas

Bananas feel soft, squishy and curved
Bananas look brown and spiky
Bananas smell good
Bananas are delicious, like apples
Bananas sound like a phone.

Kurt Cousins (7)
Allithwaite CE Primary School, Grange-Over-Sands

Obelix The Cat

When you put your ear next to him, he purrs,
He feels like a furry hairball,
He looks like a black, fluffy blanket,
He smells like a bin,
He tastes like a tooth cracking in my mouth.

Flynn Myatt (7)
Allithwaite CE Primary School, Grange-Over-Sands

Apple

A sweet taste,
Very smooth,
Round, big apple,
Red and green,
Smells good,
A big crunch!

Eleanor Ruby Horn (7)
Allithwaite CE Primary School, Grange-Over-Sands

A Smelly Cat

My cat is fat, its nose is pink, it sometimes winks,
My cat is as fluffy as a gorilla,
My cat eats birds and mice that are having a fright.
My cat's very, very bony and it feels like a stone
Without a home,
My cat smells like cat food and its tongue smells
Like a fish.
My cat's heartbeat is as loud as a stone dropping,
My cat tastes like a chicken, it's like a crisp,
But you'd better watch out for the bones!

Alistair George Hunter (6)
Allithwaite CE Primary School, Grange-Over-Sands

Cats

Cats miaowing all the time,
They smell like cat food and fish,
They are as furry as silk,
They taste really hairy,
They are as fat as a flower.

Harry Spibey (7)
Allithwaite CE Primary School, Grange-Over-Sands

One Little Kitten!

Kittens growling like elephants spraying,
Kittens walking like time,
Kittens as colourful as cheetahs,
Kittens small like a bunny,
Kittens as fluffy as a bird,
Kittens standing like meerkats,
Kittens purring like the Hoover,
Kittens talking like mice,
Kittens smelling like a portion of cat food,
Kittens tasting like juicy meat,
Kittens growling like a car,
Kittens vibrating purrs.

Mackenzie Hodgson (6)
Allithwaite CE Primary School, Grange-Over-Sands

The Mysterious Banana

Bananas smells like the sun
They smell like the moon
And the thick grass
It is as squelchy as mud
It is yellow just like you.

Lareece Pocklington (6)
Allithwaite CE Primary School, Grange-Over-Sands

My Skampi Cat

My Skampi cat feels like sheep's wool,
My Skampi cat sounds like a tractor revving up,
My Skampi cat looks like two green eyes
Moving in the dark.
My Skampi cat, smells like fish oil and fish bits,
My Skampi cat tastes like flamingoes nibbling fish.

Poppy Rose Airey (6)
Allithwaite CE Primary School, Grange-Over-Sands

Farm Senses

The farm smells like pigs.
The farm sounds like birds tweeting.
The farm looks like tractors driving.
The farm feels like blowing trees.
The farms tastes like apples.

Sam Carlin (8)
Ardnashee School & College, Londonderry

Things On A Farm

The farm smells like animals.
The farm looks like chickens laying eggs.
The farm sounds good.
The farm tastes like apples and pears.

Daisy Curry (8)
Ardnashee School & College, Londonderry

On An Expedition

I could see the hot Ribena steaming in the air,
I could smell the fishy, cold fish,
I could hear the polar bear roaring
In the snowy woods,
I could taste the salty sea splashing on my face,
I could feel the grey seal touching my nose.

Megan Hall (5)
Ashford Hill Primary School, Thatcham

We Are Going On An Expedition

I can see the ice-cold water
and it is really deep.
I can smell really hot Ribena
and it is too hot for me to drink.
I can hear the polar bear
stepping loudly in the woods.
I can taste the really hot Ribena
and it makes my tongue tingle.
I can feel the really cold and wet grass
Because I have a hole in my wellies.

Freddie James Lapham (7)
Ashford Hill Primary School, Thatcham

Going On An Expedition

I could see a fluffy wolf,
I could see an Arctic fox fishing,
I could see a slimy seal,
I could feel the ice cracking under my feet,
I could smell the warm drink,
I could feel the sheep fur in my coat,
I could see the hot Ribena bubbling in the cup,
I could see my shadow in the grass.

Arthur James Buckingham (5)
Ashford Hill Primary School, Thatcham

Going On An Expedition

I can see a fuzzy polar bear sleeping in its cave,
I can hear the snowy owl tweeting when it was flying,
I can smell the Ribena, it smells nice,
I can taste the sweet, sugary Ribena,
I can feel the wet grass and it feels freezing.

Olivia Cochrane (6)
Ashford Hill Primary School, Thatcham

Going On An Expedition

I could see the wet grass, it was very cold and
It was very white.
I could smell the polar bear, it smelt like fish,
It smelt fishy.
I could hear the polar bear growling because it was really loud.
I could feel the icy snow,
I could taste the Ribena,
I could taste the food, it was very nice,
It was fish and chips with ketchup and with beans.
I could hear the penguins flapping in the snow.
I could hear the sea lion,
I could hear the wind.

Edward Liddeatt (5)
Ashford Hill Primary School, Thatcham

Untitled

I see a polar bear,
I can smell the hot Ribena,
I can hear a husky walking,
I can taste the Ribena,
I can feel the Ribena.

Archie Thomas (6)
Ashford Hill Primary School, Thatcham

My Poem Of Senses

I can taste the sweet Ribena in the cup,
I can see the people ice fishing,
I can hear the polar bear snoring in the woods loudly,
I can smell the freezing air,
I can feel the Twix in my hands freezing.

Ariana Parkinson Gadd (6)
Ashford Hill Primary School, Thatcham

Untitled

Did you know I smell the salty sea crashing quickly against the rough, grey rocks?
I feel the wet, sloppy sand when the glistening sea crashes on my toes,
Most of the time, in the night, the lighthouse light flashes brightly in the pitch-black,
so the old, wooden boats can see.
The colourful lighthouse is as stripy as a
ziggy-zaggy zebra.
Sometimes I can see soft, cute seagulls flying high in the crystal-blue sky.
Up above I can hear miniscule, luminescent birds chirping all day,
they sing wonderful songs.
Meanwhile, I am eating warm, delicious hot dogs.
Scrumptious!

Mesha Evans (7)
Beechwood Primary School, Crewe

By The Sea

On the beach, I can feel the golden, gritty sand between my toes,
when I run towards the blue, sparkling sea.
Up above I can see some squawking,
swooping seagulls,
trying to steal people's scrumptious snacks.
Did you know that I can hear lots of waves
splashing on my feet when me and my family
run on the wet, soggy sand?
On Sunday, when I went to the amazing beach,
I saw an ice cream truck and I got some ice cream,
it was very tasty, yum yum!

Ellie-May Morris (6)
Beechwood Primary School, Crewe

Untitled

Up above my head, I can hear the scavenging,
noisy seagulls
dashing and diving and squawking. *Squawk!*
Down below my head, I can feel the wet, blue, cold water splashing, *splash!*
On the rocks, I can see all the cute, slippy
sea creatures,
talking to each other, *chat, chat!*
Over there I can smell all the lovely ice cream flavours, yum!
On the sand, I can taste the fresh green salad, delicious!

Honey Jack (6)
Beechwood Primary School, Crewe

The Beach

Down below I can feel the soft, golden sand,
squishing between my little toes as I run quickly towards the glistening, blue sea.
In-between the beach and the arcade is the fun park,
which had a slippery slide, two black swings and a bouncy horse.
Did you know that if you want a great treat,
just go to the beach and there's yummy
ice cream there?
Can you see that beautiful person swimming in
the blue sea,
she can smell pungent, salty fish jumping about.
I can hear the rough waves crashing against
the grey rocks.

Lauren Sadler (7)
Beechwood Primary School, Crewe

My Summer At The Beach

On my face I can feel the blowing, strong wind.
Next to the swishy waves I can see bumpy, small and colourful shells
that are sprinkled with gold and yellow.
Amazingly I can smell delicious hot dogs
sizzling in the frying pan in the beach cafe.
When I put a curly shell to my ear,
I can hear the big, blue sea.
Slowly, as I put my salad sandwich in my mouth,
I can taste the salty sand.

Amy Lynne Chloe Rowland (7)
Beechwood Primary School, Crewe

Untitled

Far in the distance, I can see sand swishing
across the beach,
sometimes the shells are yellow and stripy.
All the time on the rocks is the lighthouse,
we can smell the paint from it.
I can feel the sand beneath my feet,
when the soft sand goes in my mouth, I can taste it.
Slowly the wind is blowing on my face,
Slowly my feet can feel the sand.

Abbie Marie Parsonage (7)
Beechwood Primary School, Crewe

Untitled

Far in the distance there is sparkly sea splashing beneath the sky,
Down below I can see glistening sand whooshing
in the sea.
Slowly, the shining sun rises like steam from a hot cup of tasty tea.
Over there the sea crashes fiercely against
the rough rocks.

Destiny Potts (7)
Beechwood Primary School, Crewe

Paradise

Far in the distance I can see the blue, glistening waves
crash into the silvery, hard rocks.
Another thing is that I can see shiny, colourful shells
on the smooth sand.
Sometimes, when I stand on the yellow sand,
I can feel it going between my toes.
Did you know that I can smell the blue, fresh air
coming to my face?

Danikah (6)
Beechwood Primary School, Crewe

Seaside View

Far in the distance, I can see wavy, blue water
crashing against the grey rocks.
Next to the waves, I can feel sand
squishing between my toes.
Up above, I can hear six white seagulls in the air.
They are looking for yummy pizza.
Sometimes the lighthouse looks as tall as
a giraffe's neck.

Adam Strzelczyk (6)
Beechwood Primary School, Crewe

Untitled

Far in the distance, I can see glistening, blue waves crashing against the grey, jagged rocks.
Amazingly, the lighthouse is as tall as a yellow, spotty giraffe's neck..
Most of the time, the scavenging seagulls swoop
to steal a picnic sandwich.
Far away, I can smell a scrumptious, delicious and yummy hot dog. Yummy!

Quinn Dodd (7)
Beechwood Primary School, Crewe

Untitled

All of a sudden the glistening, light blue waves
crash fiercely against the brown, hard rocks!
Most of the time, I smell the yummy, scrumptious
hot dogs.
It is as hot as a brown cup of tasty tea, mmm tasty.
Did you know, the industrious lighthouse keeper
works all day,
cleaning his grimy, horrible light all day?

Whitney Wollaston (6)
Beechwood Primary School, Crewe

Tigers

Tigers sound like a snarling bear and a silent snail,
Tigers feel soft, silky and smooth,
Tigers look fit and stripy,
Tigers smell like wood, meat and the forest,
Tigers taste meaty and chewy!

Sophie Hunn (6)
Beetham CE Primary School, Milnthorpe

Ginormous Snail

Ginormous snails feel hard and slimy,
They look massive and slimy,
They sound like slithering and squirming,
They taste like beef and water,
They smell natural and earthy.

Lili Robinson (7)
Beetham CE Primary School, Milnthorpe

Trees

Trees taste of mud,
Trees smell fresh,
Trees feel bumpy,
Trees look like brown bark,
Trees sound rustly.

Grace Smith (5)
Beetham CE Primary School, Milnthorpe

Animals

I can hear a lion roar,
It feels so soft,
I can see its sharp teeth,
I can smell stinky mud!

Ted McDowell (6)
Beetham CE Primary School, Milnthorpe

A Flying Fish

I can hear flying fish crashing
and splashing into the waves,
I can feel silky and scaly bodies,
I can see shining and flying bodies,
I can smell fresh fish,
I can taste fish and chips!

Lily Sophia Christou (7)
Beetham CE Primary School, Milnthorpe

Horses And Ponies

Horses and ponies smell of shiny, shaved fur,
Horses and ponies feel amazing with a silky, soft coat,
Horses and ponies taste of hay,
Horses and ponies sound like hooves galloping
across the fields,
Horses and ponies look like little bits of shaven fur
with beautiful, glamorous eyes.

Emily Weiss (6)
Beetham CE Primary School, Milnthorpe

Under The Sea

Boats turning their way round the lake,
divers going down into the sea,
divers, divers.
Toxic seaweed hanging around the sea,
with sand in-between the rocks,
sea salt from the clams,
it's crunchy under the rocks.

Thomas Goncalves (6)
Beetham CE Primary School, Milnthorpe

Volcano

Volcanoes sound loud, like a rumbling asteroid,
Volcanoes feel hot, *ouch, ouch!*
Volcanoes look like rumbling, hot rock,
Volcanoes smell like stinky, burning-hot lava,
Volcanoes taste like hot and spicy lava.

Daniel Gardner (7)
Beetham CE Primary School, Milnthorpe

Castles, Knights, Soldiers

I can see guns and weapons,
I can smell fiery dragons,
I can taste meat,
I can feel stones,
I can hear snapping.

Maciej Piszko (6)
Beetham CE Primary School, Milnthorpe

My Poem About Space

In space it smells like oil, toxins
And fumes!
In space it looks like a gleaming, sparkly cave,
It feels like a bumpy, rough rock.
In space you can hear loud noises,
Like rocket boosters.

Holly Jenner (7)
Beetham CE Primary School, Milnthorpe

Winter

I can see falling snowflakes swirling across the sky,
I can smell very yummy chocolate cake baking, mmm!
I can hear howling winds,
I can touch the ice and cold,
I can feel frost biting my fingers, oh no!

Demi George (7)
Blueberry Park Primary School, Liverpool

Winter

I can see snowflakes blowing across the sky,
I can smell frost tickling my nose,
I can hear the stormy wind howling,
I can touch spiky, broken branches,
I feel cold and alone.

Jaden McConnon (6)
Blueberry Park Primary School, Liverpool

Winter

I can see smoke from the fire,
I can smell warm mince pie on the plate,
I can touch fluff of my blanket cover,
I can hear robins singing in the trees,
I feel snuggly in my woolly gloves.

Chloe Parker (7)
Blueberry Park Primary School, Liverpool

Winter

I can see the white clouds
I can feel the wind blowing
I can touch the snowflakes
I can hear hailstones
bashing on the roof
I can feel the frosty wind.

Connor Molloy (7)
Blueberry Park Primary School, Liverpool

Winter

I can see a big, white snowman,
I can smell fresh cookies,
I can hear the howling wind,
I can touch the slippery ice,
I feel happy and excited.

Scott Eyres (7)
Blueberry Park Primary School, Liverpool

Winter

I can see cute robins in the prickly trees,
I can smell the frost making my nose red and cold,
I can hear the brown leaves blowing in the wind,
I can touch the really prickly trees,
I feel snug in my warm coat.

Marnie Johnson (7)
Blueberry Park Primary School, Liverpool

Winter

I can see robins in the snowy trees,
I can smell frost tickling my nose,
I can hear the howling wind,
I can touch the snow when it's falling down,
I feel the slippy ice under my feet.

Kieran McMahon (7)
Blueberry Park Primary School, Liverpool

Pancake Day

I can hear pancakes popping in the pan
I can touch bumpy holes on it
I can see white sugar like white sand
I can smell a chocolatey smell
I can taste sweet, sweet sugar on it
I feel happy.

Jurek Pyszczak (5)
Blueberry Park Primary School, Liverpool

Pancake Day

I smell pancakes and jam
I taste golden honey
I touch sticky jam
I hear sizzling pancakes
I feel happy.

Ian Birnie (5)
Blueberry Park Primary School, Liverpool

Pancake Day

I smell delicious pancakes and chocolate,
The nice pancakes feel soft like flowers,
I like to eat pancakes with golden honey,
I hear pancakes popping in the pan.

Maanaswini Sabat (6)
Blueberry Park Primary School, Liverpool

The New Playground

The new playground sounds like
laughter and fun when all the
children are playing.

The new playground smells like herbs,
fresh air and excitement!

The new playground looks like wood,
swings, slides and nature.

The new playground tastes like happiness,
sunshine and surprise.

The new playground feels like
new adventures ahead...

Reception Class Miss Owens
Blueberry Park Primary School, Liverpool

Pancake Day

Pancake day
Gold honey, like the sun
I touch the pancake
I hear popping pancakes
I can taste yummy honey
I can smell sweet, yummy honey.

Lillie Taplin (5)
Blueberry Park Primary School, Liverpool

Mars Bar

The smell of delicious, silky chocolate
made my mouth water,
I'm extremely excited to rip the crunchy,
wrapped chocolate,
Gooey caramel was spilling all over my mouth,
I quickly ate my Mars bar before my mum saw me
Eating the Mars bar.
I touched the Mars bar.

Hayden Cook (7)
Blueberry Park Primary School, Liverpool

The Pink Birthday Cake

The scrumptious, pink birthday cake is sweet and strawberry flavoured,
I can smell a blast of strawberries coming from the
big, pink cake,
The cake had seven lit candles,
It was like a party in my mouth.

Keeley Hart (6)
Blueberry Park Primary School, Liverpool

The Spotty Cheetah

The cheetah ran fast, like a flash,
I was in a forest with lots of animals,
When the cheetah ran fast smoke went in my face,
It went in my mouth, it tasted yucky.
I walked along the scary forest and I stopped,
I heard a noise, it sounded like an elephant,
Phew! It went away,
So I walked along,
I smelled some yucky food, yuck!

Summer Jones (6)
Blueberry Park Primary School, Liverpool

Untitled

When my dad cooked my pancake
the pancake was popping in my mouth,
it was hot.
It smelt nice,
I could hear popping,
It smelt good and fresh,
I could feel that it was soft.

Vanesa Libakova (5)
Blueberry Park Primary School, Liverpool

My Mum Made Some Pancakes

Pancakes taste good,
Pancakes smell nice,
Pancakes sound sizzling,
Pancakes feel spongy,
Pancakes look brown and holey and crunchy,
Pancakes feel hot and chewy,
Pancakes sound slimy and popping,
They taste gorgeous
And they smell beautiful and look tiny.

Kyle Williams (5)
Blueberry Park Primary School, Liverpool

Pirate

I can see some footprints in the sand,
the smell of salty seaweed is floating up my nose.
The sweet taste of coconut in my mouth,
I can touch smooth, yellow sand,
soft as fluffy cushions,
waves are washing and crashing on the rocks,
happiness makes me move around.

Oscar Sell (7)
Blueberry Park Primary School, Liverpool

The Cheetah

I saw a cheetah, it zoomed like the wind,
I could not believe I got to ride him.
He ran fast and so hot,
He saw a den to cool him down,
We laid down together and closed our eyes.

Phillip Joseph Lynch (7)
Blueberry Park Primary School, Liverpool

I Love Pancake Day

Pancake Day is a special day,
Pancakes taste like lemon,
'Mom, I want cream on it.'
Pancakes look brown and spotty.

Neriah Anthony (6)
Blueberry Park Primary School, Liverpool

Yummy Pancakes

My mummy put the pancakes in the pan,
I heard the pan sizzling.
My mummy touched the pancakes, they were roasting,
My pancake was soft,
My mum tried the pancakes
And they were nice.
My mummy smelt the pancakes
And my mummy saw brown pancakes.

Verity Cook (5)
Blueberry Park Primary School, Liverpool

Untitled

One day my mum went to make some pancakes,
they looked delicious,
they smelt good and they felt fantastic.
They were flat and they were special.

Emily Jayde Tague (6)
Blueberry Park Primary School, Liverpool

Mum's Pancakes

When my mum cooks pancakes
they are sweet,
they smell tasty,
they taste good and look yummy.
I can hear sizzling in the pan,
they taste crunchy.
In the pan the pancakes were sizzling very much.

Scott Courtney Ashworth (6)
Blueberry Park Primary School, Liverpool

Pancake Senses

I hear popping.
I can see the pancake.
I can smell bubbling.
I can taste the chocolate.
I can feel them in my tummy.

Joshua Clark (6)
Broughton Primary School, Cockermouth

Pancake Senses

I can hear it bubbling
I can see chocolate melting on my pancake
I can smell bananas and kiwis
I can taste sweetness
I can feel it going down my throat.

Holly Graham (6)
Broughton Primary School, Cockermouth

Pancake Poem

P ancakes popping in the pan
A nd I hear them sizzle
N ext flip the pancake
C atch it if you can
A nd put the pancake on the plate
K eep on eating as fast as you can
E veryone loves pancakes
S queeze your lemon.

Willow Richardson (6)
Broughton Primary School, Cockermouth

Pancake Poem

P ancakes popping,
A nd sizzling in the pan,
N ow I add my tasty toppings,
C hocolate melting on my pancake,
A nd my syrup is delicious on my pancake,
K eep eating until I get full,
E ach day I eat pancakes and they taste delicious.

Sophia Tzelepi-Jones (5)
Broughton Primary School, Cockermouth

Pancake Senses

I can hear them popping and banging.
I can see the flying pancake.
I can smell the Nutella.
I can taste brilliant bananas.
I can feel it in my tummy.

Shay Williams (6)
Broughton Primary School, Cockermouth

Pancake Poem

P op the pancake in the pan
A nd watch the pancake in the pan sizzling
N ext flip the pancake
C atch if you can
A ll can smell the syrup
K eep on eating till you're full
E veryone likes pancakes
S crumptious pancakes in my tummy.

Samantha Hewitt (6)
Broughton Primary School, Cockermouth

Pancake Senses

I can hear the pancake popping.
I can see my daddy flip the pan.
I can smell the pancake bubbling in the pan.
I can taste the gooey mixture in my tummy.
I can feel it slipping down my throat.

Millie Rose Graham (5)
Broughton Primary School, Cockermouth

Pancake Poem

P op the pancake in the pan.
A nd watch the pancake bubble.
N ext you flip the pancake over.
C atch it if you can!
A mazing it looks, I say.
K eep munching as fast as you can.
E veryone loves pancakes!
S queeze all the pancake in your tummy.

Lexie Hutchinson (5)
Broughton Primary School, Cockermouth

Pancakes

Flip the pan
Catch the pancake if you can!
That looks yummy
Get in my tummy
Sniff the pancake cooking in the pan
I'm so hot I need a fan
I can't wait to taste the topping
I just wish it would stop popping!
The pancake tastes like a dream
Now quick get me the cream!

Kian Michael Tyson (5)
Broughton Primary School, Cockermouth

Pancake Poem

P op the pancake on the plate
A nd hear it crunching
N ext fling the pancake in the air
C atch it if you can
A nd I can smell the chocolate
K eep eating until you are full
E at all of it up
S ame every year.

Ewan Abraham (6)
Broughton Primary School, Cockermouth

Pancake Senses

I can hear it pop, pop, pop
I can see it cooking.
I can smell melting chocolate.
I can taste chocolate.
I can feel it's sticky.

Charleigh Taylor (6)
Broughton Primary School, Cockermouth

Pancake Poem

P ancake popping in the pan
A nd you flip it
N ext flip the pancake in the air
C atch it if you can!
A nd smell the pancake in the
K itchen
E at your pancake. It is
S crumptious!

Alexander Murray (6)
Broughton Primary School, Cockermouth

Pancake Poem

P ancakes popping in the pan.
A nd sizzling in the pan.
N ow I can add my tasty toppings.
C hocolate melting on my pancake.
A nd my syrup tastes like sugar.
K eep eating until I am full.
E ach year I have pancakes.

Bethany Lauren Bebb (6)
Broughton Primary School, Cockermouth

Peaceful Scotland

In bonny Scotland hooting bagpipes are played in
the bustling streets.
I can feel the cold river trickling under
the ragged bridge.
I can see red deer jumping on the hills in the sunset.
I can smell lovely flowers growing in the valley.
I can taste haggis fresh from the busy shops.
What a really lovely place.

Catriona Lilian Bell (7)
Cartmel CE Primary School, Grange-Over-Sands

Beautiful Scotland

I can smell the breeze of Scotland.
Scotland sounds like splendid birds
speaking in the morning.
Scotland tastes like haggis chomping in your mouth.
Scotland looks like a beautiful place.
Scotland feels all nice and tingly inside you.
Scotland is beautiful.
The bagpipes banging along the street!

Charlie Crabtree (7)
Cartmel CE Primary School, Grange-Over-Sands

Scotland

Leaves crunching on the lovely soil.
Tasting porridge swirling in the bowl.
I can hear birds tweeting in the trees.
I can smell delicious hot chocolate.
I can smell juicy pineapple.
I can see beautiful shooting stars.
I can hear hooting bagpipes.
I can see ants.
The sea moves.
Scotland is spectacular and amazing!

Henry Crabtree (7)
Cartmel CE Primary School, Grange-Over-Sands

Scotland Is The Best

It looks like a little mouse
It tastes like lovely fish
I can feel a flower
I love the smell of nature
I love the sound of water.

Ollie Hunter-Lowe (7)
Cartmel CE Primary School, Grange-Over-Sands

Untitled

I can hear the birds singing in the extraordinary sunset
I can feel the stream swirling
I can feel the sun shining in the wind
I can hear the fireworks flying together
I can smell roses
I can hear the guitar playing
I can hear the ferries sailing by.

Brooke Coward (5)
Cartmel CE Primary School, Grange-Over-Sands

The Cool Scotland

Scotland smells like delicious porridge
Scotland sounds like delightful birds singing
Scotland looks like the roaring sea
Scotland feels like the amazing sea.

James Robert Bland (6)
Cartmel CE Primary School, Grange-Over-Sands

Baking A Cake

I love to bake a cake,
Because it is fun to make,
When I pour the flour it makes me sneeze,
But bubbling butter is a delightful breeze,
The humming of the oven and the rattling of the whisk,
I am sure I am not taking a risk.
When I smell the chocolate it makes me hungry,
But when I try the condensed milk it
sometimes tastes funny.

Keya Shona Mistry (6)
Edge Grove School, Watford

On A Pirate Ship

I see pirates duelling and climbing the rigging.
I can feel sharp hooks and rough swords.
I can smell rotten codfish and stinking socks.
I can taste sweet rum and salty sea water.
I can hear hooks banging and swords clanging.
I can hear parrots squawking.

Kyan Peter Bhupendra Mehta (5)
Edge Grove School, Watford

Morning At The Museum

My chocolate biscuits were so yummy,
They filled my tummy,
The rocks were bumpy,
My hands got so lumpy,
The dinosaur bones were a bit scary,
But also made me merry,
The velociraptor was roaring,
It sounded like snoring,
The sweet flowers,
As tall as towers.

Mohammed Ali Reza (6)
Edge Grove School, Watford

Seaside

Stand by the sea,
What can you hear?
The gulls and horns,
as they screech in my ear.
Dip your feet in the water,
what do you feel?
The squishy sand and the wet, cold water,
tickling my heel.
Sit on the jetty,
what can you smell?
The whiff of the yummy fish and chips,
spreading its magical spell.
Walk on the beach,
what can you taste?
The salty ocean air,
stinging my face.
Lie on the golden sand,
what can you see?
The big bright sky,
looking down at me.

Dara Olunloyo (6)
Edge Grove School, Watford

Garden Sight In Spring

Outside my window I see,
Bright yellow daffodils,
as bright as the sun!
The brightness in the sky,
as light as a blue dragonfly!
The fence as smooth as a wooden toy.
The spring has come, oh joy!

Fatemah Asaria (5)
Edge Grove School, Watford

Surfboards And Chips

The sun shines and rises,
The salt is tasty,
I can feel my board,
And smell fish,
As I ride the waves,
I eat chips.

Archer Francis Kettle (5)
Edge Grove School, Watford

Grandma's Kitchen

Fred lives here
Fred is a goldfish
We make cupcakes here
We put sprinkles on them
And chocolate
I want to eat them all up
But not Fred.

Isabella Little (5)
Edge Grove School, Watford

The Best Home

This is the best home.
I touch teddy, crayons and foam.
I hear my baby brother crying.
I taste food that is good for eating.
I smell food on the smoky barbecue.
I see pencils, paper and you.
Thank you for listening to my poem,
about my home.

Ehije Izzi-Engbeaya (5)
Edge Grove School, Watford

Friends

I can see something in the sky and it is
a fluttering butterfly.
Sun and rainbow dancing in the sky.
We are dancing and having some fun.
We are making snowmen together,
and playing with toys.
We read the books and sing the songs.
We pretend that we are the band,
we play musical instruments.
After a long playtime when we are tired.
We share pizza and cakes, that makes our day.

Francesca Mackenzie (5)
Edge Grove School, Watford

Lego!

Lego is made of plastic
To play it is fantastic
I love to play with Lego
I love to use the yellow.

Joel Abraham Jaffe (6)
Edge Grove School, Watford

Josh

I hear Josh crying in the morning to get up.
He then eats his breakfast messily.
When he gets dressed his hair goes fluffy.
He smiles with his chubby cheeks.
But then we smell his pooey nappy!

Caitlin O'Keeffe (6)
Edge Grove School, Watford

Lala

Lala is my bunny,
she's cuddly like my mummy.
She has a soft pink nose,
and fluffy toes.
She smells delicious,
very chocolicious.
I love Lala.

Charlotte Mai Gardiner (6)
Edge Grove School, Watford

Fire!

Help my street is on fire!
People are screaming!
When will the fire engines be here?
I can hear them, but I can't see them.
I can see cinders swirling up in the clouds.
I can hear horns going.
I feel hot and I can taste bitter smoke.

Evan Nursiah (6)
Edge Grove School, Watford

Noisy Tractor

I was driving the noisy tractor one day,
I cut the hedge and the grass,
It smelt good,
Driving along the grey road,
I can feel the vibration on the steering wheel
I can smell the fresh air,
But the engine is very smoky.

Hugh Padayachy (6)
Edge Grove School, Watford

Holiday

I see the sea and sand,
I taste the pizza and chocolate pancakes,
I smell and touch the hot sand,
And I hear the waves shushing.

Amber Hilton (5)
Edge Grove School, Watford

Ella, My Super-Duper Best Friend

What makes me happy?
Ella Bella Boo, my best friend!
When I hear her say funny things,
She makes me laugh.
When she gives me a big hug,
She makes me feel loved,
When I can see her,
I feel excited at the thought of playing,
Her cupcakes are the best to taste.
How does she smell?
With her nose of course!
And that's Ella Bella Boo, my best friend.

Kimaya Kapadia (6)
Edge Grove School, Watford

Your poem has been chosen as the best in this book!

Me, My House And My Home

I could see Mummy's cooking books on the bookshelf,
Mummy on the sofa, Daddy putting up pictures,
Daddy on the laptop, Mummy on the iPad.
I love the taste of pizza, toast and Nutella,
I could feel the table, pencil and flowers around me,
I could smell myself, air freshener and
flowers in my home,
I could hear the TV and Daddy talking in
the living room.

Zachary Oladuji (5)
Edge Grove School, Watford

The Zoo

At the zoo I smelt animal poo.
I touched a goat, he was fluffy.
I saw a crocodile.

Honor
Edge Grove School, Watford

Forest School

Forest School is fun because,
I like rolling in muddy puddles.
I like forest school because,
I like climbing trees.
I like Forest School because,
I like jumping in muddy puddles.
I like making things at Forest School.

Eniola Opaleye (6)
Edge Grove School, Watford

The Great Barrier Reef

If I went diving in the Great Barrier Reef...
I might see small, beautiful fish looking for tasty food.
I might hear waves crashing on the rocks.
I might smell the salty, slimy seaweed.
I might feel the beautiful, rough coral as I swim over it.
I might taste the salty, blue sea.

Alfie Ayres (6)
Fairfield Primary School, Stockton-On-Tees

The Great Barrier Reef

If I went diving in the Great Barrier Reef...
I might see a school of tropical colourful fish and massive sea turtles gliding through the coral.
I might hear a pod of dolphins singing beautifully as they swim gently.
I might smell the green, wet seaweed
as I swim around.
I might feel the beautiful, scaly fish
swimming around my feet.
I might taste the disgusting sea water in my mouth.

Alexa Grace Wiley (6)
Fairfield Primary School, Stockton-On-Tees

The Great Barrier Reef

If I went diving in the Great Barrier Reef...
I might see a pink anemone where clown fish live and other lovely coral.
I might hear colourful parrot fish nibbling the rocks.
I might smell the horrible, salty sea air.
I might touch the slimy coral while I look at
a pod of dolphins.
I might taste the horrible sea water.

Joseph Watson (7)
Fairfield Primary School, Stockton-On-Tees

The Great Barrier Reef

If I went diving in the Great Barrier Reef...
I might see a beautiful clown fish popping out of its sea anemone.
I might smell the ink from an octopus glowing brightly.
I might hear bubbles popping and a pod of dolphins singing elegantly around me.
I might touch a very scaly sea snake.
I might taste the salty air.

Alexander Gaskell (7)
Fairfield Primary School, Stockton-On-Tees

The Great Barrier Reef

If I went diving in the Great Barrier Reef...
I might see beautiful, tropical fish gliding towards me.
I might hear the amazing waves crashing on the rocks.
I might touch the rough rocks and sea snails.
I might taste the ice cream after my
underwater adventure.

Thomas Mbabazi (6)
Fairfield Primary School, Stockton-On-Tees

The Great Barrier Reef

If I went diving in the Great Barrier Reef...
I might see a school of bright, colourful fish swimming away from a terrifying great white shark.
I might hear a pod of dolphins
singing elegantly around me.
I might smell the green, salty seaweed.
I might touch the curly-whirly coral as
I swim around it.
I might taste a lovely vanilla ice cream after my fantastic adventure.

Summer Gibb (7)
Fairfield Primary School, Stockton-On-Tees

The Great Barrier Reef

If I went diving in the Great Barrier Reef...
I might see wonderful, tropical fish swimming away from a terrifying shark.
I might hear boats travelling over the lovely coral reef.
I might smell the fresh, salty sea air.
I might feel the lovely, curly, beautiful coral.
I might taste the bubbly bubbles that were
popping around me.

Xenia Rose Parry (6)
Fairfield Primary School, Stockton-On-Tees

The Great Barrier Reef

If I went diving in the Great Barrier Reef...
I might see an enormous, scary shark looking for its tasty food and chasing after it really fast.
I might hear noisy boat engines as they travel
through the sea.
I might smell the stinky seaweed stuck to the rocks.
I might touch the slimy and squishy coral but I would have to be very careful.
I might taste the salty underwater sea world.

Oliver David John Fish (6)
Fairfield Primary School, Stockton-On-Tees

The Great Barrier Reef

If I went diving in the Great Barrier Reef...
I might see the rainbow, tropical fish in
the beautiful ocean.
I might hear the parrot fish chomping on hard rocks.
I might smell the fresh, salty sea air.
I might feel the soggy, wet seaweed around me.
I might taste the beautiful ice cream after a long trip.

Ruby Dinsdale (6)
Fairfield Primary School, Stockton-On-Tees

The Great Barrier Reef

If I went diving in the Great Barrier Reef...
I might see beautiful, coloured fish
swimming around me.
I might hear the dancing bubbles popping on
the sharp rocks.
I might smell the fresh, salty sea.
I might touch the shells that are on the sea floor.
I might taste a chocolate ice cream on the boat.

Phoebe Carr Armson (6)
Fairfield Primary School, Stockton-On-Tees

The Great Barrier Reef

If I went diving in the Great Barrier Reef...
I might see a school of tropical fish and jellyfish.
I might hear a pod of dolphins swimming around.
I might feel the squishy coral under me but watch out – it might tickle!
I might taste the salty sea water and the seaweed.

Olivia Hobbs (7)
Fairfield Primary School, Stockton-On-Tees

The Great Barrier Reef

If I went diving in the Great Barrier Reef...
I might see tropical fish getting chased by a gang of ferocious, hungry sharks.
I might hear the red snapping crabs
catching their dinner.
I might smell the fresh, salty sea air.
I might feel the octopuses' suckers, sucking my feet.
I might taste a delicious ice cream on the boat.

Lucy Robertson (6)
Fairfield Primary School, Stockton-On-Tees

The Great Barrier Reef

If I went diving in the Great Barrier Reef...
I might see a school of tropical fish swimming to
the drop-off.
I might hear the bubbles in the sea.
I might smell the slimy seaweed.
I might touch a big shark with sharp teeth.
I might taste the salty water in my mask and
the yucky seaweed.

Levi Graham (7)
Fairfield Primary School, Stockton-On-Tees

The Great Barrier Reef

If I went diving in the Great Barrier Reef...
I might see the colourful coral and rainbow fish
in the reef.
I might hear the singing dolphins as they
glide past me.
I might smell the fresh, salty sea air.
I might touch the spiky coral as I look at all the fish.
I might taste the salty sea.

Joseph Hall (6)
Fairfield Primary School, Stockton-On-Tees

The Great Barrier Reef

If I went diving in the Great Barrier Reef...
I might see hungry, terrifying sharks looking for terrified sea turtles and tropical fish swimming fast.
I might hear long sea snakes swimming around me.
I might smell the beautiful fish swimming past me.
I might touch the slimy sea snakes and
the spiky starfish.
I might taste the delicious ice lollies after a fantastic water adventure.

Harvey Knowles (6)
Fairfield Primary School, Stockton-On-Tees

The Great Barrier Reef

If I went diving in the Great Barrier Reef...
I might see the beautiful tropical fish under the reef.
I might hear a pod of dolphins, sweetly singing as they gently glide around me.
I might smell the salty, fresh air and the slimy seaweed.
I might touch the shiny coral and the slippery dolphins.
I might taste the gorgeous ice cream when we get out of the salty sea.

Holly Cotton (6)
Fairfield Primary School, Stockton-On-Tees

The Great Barrier Reef

If I went diving in the Great Barrier Reef...
I might see scary sharks looking for their prey and a huge whale shark swimming past.
I might hear a pod of dolphins sweetly singing while swimming over me.
I might smell the salty sea air as I swim around.
I might touch the very rough clams.
I might taste the salty sea while I
swim back to the boat.

Finley Moody (6)
Fairfield Primary School, Stockton-On-Tees

The Great Barrier Reef

If I went diving in the Great Barrier Reef...
I might see a school of moonfish getting chased by hungry hammerhead sharks.
I might hear the red crab's pincers snapping on
the hard rocks.
I might smell the fresh, salty sea air.
I might feel the fabulous, scaly fish
swimming around the reef.
I might taste the fresh air from my sky above.

Evie Pearce (7)
Fairfield Primary School, Stockton-On-Tees

The Great Barrier Reef

If I went diving in the Great Barrier Reef...
I might see a school of tropical fish
swimming in the bright reef.
I might hear a colourful parrotfish nibbling the rocks.
I might smell the smelly, salty sea.
I might touch the colourful, tropical fish.
I might taste the grilled fish on the barbecue
after my adventure.

Charlie George Clough (6)
Fairfield Primary School, Stockton-On-Tees

The Great Barrier Reef

If I went diving in the Great Barrier Reef...
I might see a herd of fierce hammerhead sharks.
I might hear a whale calling for its young.
I might smell the fresh, salty sea air.
I might feel the slime from an enormous sea snake swimming towards me.
I might taste a scrumptious, ice-cold drink after an amazing day.

Daniel O'Keeffe (7)
Fairfield Primary School, Stockton-On-Tees

The Great Barrier Reef

If I went diving in the Great Barrier Reef...
I might see a glowing jellyfish and other tropical fish swimming in the fantastic coral.
I might hear dangerous snapping sharks
coming towards me.
I might smell the fresh, salty sea air.
I might touch the beautifully coloured coral and the tickling, slimy seaweed in-between my toes.
I might taste the disgusting seaweed.

Ayva Wilde (6)
Fairfield Primary School, Stockton-On-Tees

The Great Barrier Reef

If I went diving in the Great Barrier Reef...
I might see a red octopus swimming and a
wiggling jellyfish.
I might hear a parrotfish crunching on colourful coral.
I might smell the salty sea.
I might the spiky starfish under my toes.
I might taste the salty sea water
coming through my mask.

Anna Lin (7)
Fairfield Primary School, Stockton-On-Tees

The Great Barrier Reef

If I went diving in the Great Barrier Reef...
I might see a school of tropical fish about to be eaten by a huge shark.
I might hear the dolphins swimming around me, singing beautifully.
I might smell the delicious ice cream
from the boat above.
I might feel the beautiful, amazing coral tickling me as I hunt for baby sea turtles.
I might taste a scrumptious ice cream on the deck of the beautiful boat.

Alfie Brown (6)
Fairfield Primary School, Stockton-On-Tees

The Great Barrier Reef

If I went diving in the Great Barrier Reef...
I might see a bloom of blue, beautiful jellyfish,
I might smell the lovely, salty sea,
I might hear squids going *splodge, splodge*.
I might touch a sea turtle swimming in the
crystal-blue water,
I might taste the salty sea.

Lucy Banthorpe (6)
Fairfield Primary School, Stockton-On-Tees

The Great Barrier Reef

If I went diving in the Great Barrier Reef...
I might see a hermit crab pinching
another diver's finger!
I might smell octopus ink a mile away because the ink is so strong.
I might hear a reef shark munching on a school of fish.
I might touch a wonderful, pink jellyfish gliding through the crystal-clear water.
I might taste the salty sea.

Zachary Clark (6)
Fairfield Primary School, Stockton-On-Tees

The Great Barrier Reef

If I went diving in the Great Barrier Reef...
I might see a blue, shiny dolphin
playing with her children.
I might smell the nice coral smelling like perfume.
I might hear the clumsy dolphins
jumping and squeaking.
I might touch a gorgeous, little baby dolphin, when it is swimming with its mum.
I might taste the fish food coming through my mask.

Aimee Dixon (7)
Fairfield Primary School, Stockton-On-Tees

The Great Barrier Reef

If I went diving in the Great Barrier Reef...
I might see a crystal-blue dolphin playing ball with other shiny dolphins.
I might smell the coral smelling like perfume, it is waving at some shells.
I might hear the bubbles popping.
I might touch a turtle with a baby turtle in the amazing, fabulous coral eating some delicious food.
I might taste some salty sand and fish food.

Alice Osborne (6)
Fairfield Primary School, Stockton-On-Tees

The Great Barrier Reef

If I went diving in the Great Barrier Reef...
I might see a green bloom of jellyfish.
I might smell an evil-eyed, strange-looking octopus, with a bad temper.
I might hear an octopus spraying ink.
I might touch an adorable sea turtle
swimming in the water.
I might taste sea biscuits that are yucky.

Arden Stephens (7)
Fairfield Primary School, Stockton-On-Tees

The Great Barrier Reef

If I went diving in the Great Barrier Reef...
I might see cool crabs snapping under the sea.
I might touch a powerful tiger fish, it's very powerful
to protect itself.
I might smell the powerful black ink from an octopus.
I might hear the amazing crabs snapping.
I might taste some black ink from an octopus.

Callum Lane-Tingle (7)
Fairfield Primary School, Stockton-On-Tees

The Great Barrier Reef

If I went diving in the Great Barrier Reef...
I might see a great white shark sneaking up on a school of fish next to some colourful, purple coral.
I might smell the red, sticky blood from a grey and white shark's teeth.
I might hear the black ink squirt from
an angry octopus.
I might touch a great white shark.
I might taste the blue, crystal-clear water.

Benjamin O'Donnell (7)
Fairfield Primary School, Stockton-On-Tees

The Great Barrier Reef

If I went diving in the Great Barrier Reef...
I might see some great white sharks chasing colourful, white and orange clownfish.
I might smell some disgusting ink from
a purple octopus.
I might hear loads of popping bubbles
and waves crashing.
I might taste the ink from a squid and salty water.
I might touch the dolphins that are hugging me.

Grace Nelson (7)
Fairfield Primary School, Stockton-On-Tees

The Great Barrier Reef

If I went diving in the Great Barrier Reef...
I might see a pufferfish who might be
angry and greedy.
I might smell the sharks' smelly teeth and see it chasing some fish.
I might hear the engine of a boat that is
moving very fast.
I might touch the seaweed, gently swaying about and a clownfish in an anemone.
I might taste ink from an orange octopus,
and seaweed.

Grace Warnock (6)
Fairfield Primary School, Stockton-On-Tees

The Great Barrier Reef

If I went diving in the Great Barrier Reef...
I might see clownfish swimming out of the beautiful, amazing anemone.
I might smell the tropical fish food.
I might hear the great white shark chomping on some colourful coral.
I might touch the colourful, tropical fish
eating fish food.
I might taste some disgusting sea water and air
from my mask.

Hayden Kenning (7)
Fairfield Primary School, Stockton-On-Tees

The Great Barrier Reef

If I went diving in the Great Barrier Reef...
I might hear a shark chomping on a group of tropical fish and a swordfish fighting with a stingray.
I might smell the jellyfish and the squishy, soft coral and the hunting shark.
I might taste the coral and shark blood.
I might see a big, huge swordfish and a huge, giant whale shark hunting a giant crab.
I might touch a dangerous swordfish
and some picturesque fish.

Jacob Reed (6)
Fairfield Primary School, Stockton-On-Tees

The Great Barrier Reef

If I went diving in the Great Barrier Reef...
I might see a reef shark chasing after a school of fish with shimmery, shiny scales.
I might smell a stinky crab being chased by a horrible great white shark, which has a fish stuck in its teeth.
I might hear sharks fighting over a juicy fish.
I might touch a jellyfish floating gently in the crystal-blue ocean and it might nearly sting me and also touch some amazing, silky angelfish.
I might taste the salty, stinking salt water
and bubbles popping.

Jacob Edward Riley (7)
Fairfield Primary School, Stockton-On-Tees

The Great Barrier Reef

If I went diving in the Great Barrier Reef...
I might smell the bottom of a wooden boat.
I might hear the waves crashing.
I might touch the golden sandy seabed.
I might taste the salty water.

Joseph White (7)
Fairfield Primary School, Stockton-On-Tees

The Great Barrier Reef

If I went diving in the Great Barrier Reef...
I might see a huge great white shark chasing after thousands of fish.
I might smell the smelly, stinky poo of the fish.
I might hear the loud, scary howling of a whale.
I might touch colourful, shiny coral and a huge turtle gliding like a bird.
I might taste the smelly, nice perfume of the
colourful, shiny coral.

Kallan Joe Robert Mason (7)
Fairfield Primary School, Stockton-On-Tees

The Great Barrier Reef

If I went diving in the Great Barrier Reef...
I might see the beautiful coral on the seabed.
I might hear the sharks fighting.
I might touch some sharks.
I might taste the bubbles from my mask.

Joseph Edward Wrigley (6)
Fairfield Primary School, Stockton-On-Tees

The Great Barrier Reef

If I went diving in the Great Barrier Reef...
I might see a group of stingrays
chasing me with their tails.
I might smell the horrible fish poo – I wouldn't like the disgusting, stinky smell of it!
I might hear the crashing waves, moving in the crystal-clear, open, blue sea.
I might touch a bunch of beautiful, colourful coral.
I might taste some fish food.

Kane Warrick (6)
Fairfield Primary School, Stockton-On-Tees

The Great Barrier Reef

If I went diving in the Great Barrier Reef...
I might smell the tropical, scaly fish.
I might hear the bubbles popping in the water.
I might touch a powerful electric eel and
the salty sand.
I might taste sea biscuits.

Lincoln Miles Benjamin White (6)
Fairfield Primary School, Stockton-On-Tees

The Great Barrier Reef

If I went diving in the Great Barrier Reef...
I might see a great white shark with shiny, white teeth.
I might smell the colourful, gorgeous coral with
goldfish in it.
I might hear the waves crashing with fury.
I might touch an amazing turtle in a place with
other magnificent turtles.
I might taste disgusting fish food.

Katie Rose Morris (7)
Fairfield Primary School, Stockton-On-Tees

The Great Barrier Reef

If I went diving in the Great Barrier Reef...
I might see tropical fish.
I might hear crabs snapping their claws.
I might smell the salty sea in the reef.
I might touch a big, shiny sea turtle
gliding through the water.
I might taste the salty sea and the seaweed.

Lucas Harley Elliott (6)
Fairfield Primary School, Stockton-On-Tees

The Great Barrier Reef

If I went diving in the Great Barrier Reef...
I might see a bloom of glowing, bright jellyfish. Also, a pufferfish at the back.
I might smell a shark's teeth with blood on it and a blue-ringed octopus!
I might hear the lovely, beautiful dolphins diving!
I might touch the cool, wriggly, amazing coral.
I might taste some yummy, lovely, salty sea water.

Millie Eve Gibbon (7)
Fairfield Primary School, Stockton-On-Tees

The Great Barrier Reef

If I went diving in the Great Barrier Reef...
I might see a group of tropical fish
swimming up to me.
I might touch a whale shark swimming up to me and beautiful rock fish
swimming away from a
great white shark.
I might smell a great white shark chasing after a bloom of jellyfish.
I might hear an anemone, swaying in the water.
I might taste some amazing fish bubbles.

Payton Grace Goodhall (7)
Fairfield Primary School, Stockton-On-Tees

The Great Barrier Reef

If I went diving in the Great Barrier Reef...
I might see a smelly sea snail slithering around.
I might smell the beautiful, yummy smell of the coral.
I might hear tropical, colourful, small fish wriggling their tails.
I might touch a pink, amazing starfish!
I might taste the smelly, stinky, disgusting seaweed.

Ben Rutter (6)
Fairfield Primary School, Stockton-On-Tees

Our Wonderful World

I can see the ice-cold and red lava volcano.
I can hear a lamb baaing.
I can smell the flowers.
I can taste the sweet carrots.
I can touch the fluffy lambs.

Paige Reed (5)
Hillcroft Primary School, Caterham

Our Wonderful World

I can see the beautiful purple flowers and the volcano fire exploding.
I can hear the dolphin squeaking and lightning rumbling and crashing.
I can smell the salty sea and the rain.
I can taste the orange, juicy carrot and the
soft, yellow banana.
I can touch a soft, smooth chick and soft snow.

Veenaa Kistnen (6)
Hillcroft Primary School, Caterham

Our Wonderful World

I can see an orange volcano.
I can hear loud thunder.
I can smell flowers.
I can taste carrot.
I can touch a hard stone.

Kyle Cheeseman (6)
Hillcroft Primary School, Caterham

Our Wonderful World

I can see a mean tiger.
I can hear a hooting owl.
I can smell a flower.
I can taste banana.
I can touch a smooth conker.

Alexz Davis (6)
Hillcroft Primary School, Caterham

Our Wonderful World

I can see a colourful, noisy peacock.
I can hear a cheeping chick cheeping.
I can smell the lovely-smelling flowers.
I can taste the cold, soft snow on my tongue.
I can touch the white, soft lamb.

Jessica Drew Grant (6)
Hillcroft Primary School, Caterham

Our Wonderful World

I can see the black and orange furry tiger in the
metal black cage.
I can hear the frightening thunder, crashing through the black, silent sky.
I can smell the fresh air and wind
swirling through the trees.
I can touch the squishy, yellow custard and
the hard rocks.
I can taste the soft, yellow banana and the
ripe, red apple.

Daisy Patton (6)
Hillcroft Primary School, Caterham

Our Wonderful World

I can see colourful fish.
I can hear cracking lightning.
I can smell salty sea.
I can taste a carrot.
I can touch soft birds.

Ethan Russell (5)
Hillcroft Primary School, Caterham

Our Wonderful World

I can see cold, clear ice.
I can hear a perfect parrot.
I can smell the salty sea.
I can taste a yummy banana.
I can touch the spiky cactus.

Ben David Hoey (6)
Hillcroft Primary School, Caterham

Our Wonderful World

I can see lovely flowers and
I can hear loud thunder
I can smell delicious cookies and
I can taste delicious chocolate
I can touch soft snow.

Bella Hill (5)
Hillcroft Primary School, Caterham

Our Wonderful World

I can see clear, cold ice in the arctic.
I can hear strong waves.
I can smell wavy flowers.
I can taste cold snow on my lip.
I can touch the warm, wet sea.

Stanley Hopkins (6)
Hillcroft Primary School, Caterham

Our Wonderful World

I can see a colourful peacock.
I can hear clicking dolphins.
I can smell purple lavender.
I can taste a yellow banana.
I can touch a spiky cactus.

Jake Fuller (5)
Hillcroft Primary School, Caterham

Our Wonderful World

I can see a stripy tiger.
I can hear jingle bells.
I can smell the salty sea.
I can taste a chocolate cookie.
I can touch a spiky cactus.

Blaine Paterson (6)
Hillcroft Primary School, Caterham

Our Wonderful World

I can see a red, fiery volcano.
I can hear the loud lightning in the air.
I can smell the water in the sea.
I can taste the cold ice in the arctic.
I can touch the warm sea and cold sea.

Amelia Krawczyk (6)
Hillcroft Primary School, Caterham

Our Wonderful World

I can see the beautiful, shimmery stars up in the sky and a little yellow chick.
I can hear the hooting owls up in the trees and the wind blowing in my ear.
I can smell the beautiful flowers up in the meadow and the salty blue sea.
I can taste the ripe, red apples up in the trees.
I can touch the hard rocks in my hand and
the spiky cactus.

Kacie Anders (6)
Hillcroft Primary School, Caterham

Our Wonderful World

I can see my friends playing Minecraft.
I can hear loud lightning.
I can smell bananas.
I can taste an orange.
I can touch money.

Samuel Read (5)
Hillcroft Primary School, Caterham

Our Wonderful World

I can see the beach.
I can hear the splashy dolphin.
I can smell lavender.
I can taste carrots.
I can touch a green cactus.

George Wilson (5)
Hillcroft Primary School, Caterham

Cupcakes

I hear the oven go *ping*
My cupcakes are done
The smell of lovely vanilla extract
Hops into my nose
They feel fluffy and spongy
Once they are decorated they look like
they are ballerinas
The strawberry icing and vanilla icing
Taste absolutely delicious
I love cupcakes!

Aditi Gampa (6)
King's House Preparatory School & Nursery, Luton

My Mama

My mama looks like a beautiful princess
In her glamorous shoes and her bright, yellow dress.

My mama smells like cake and pretty flowers
She smells so beautiful, I could sniff her for hours!

My mama sounds like a bird chirping
happily in its nest
Her singing sounds so lovely, when it's at its very best.

My mama feels as warm as fluffy teddy bears
Her cuddles makes me feel that she
really, really cares!

My mama tastes like strawberries and cream
She tastes as delicious as an amazing dream!

Without my mama, I would scream!

Ava May Rossiter (7)
King's House Preparatory School & Nursery, Luton

A Poem About Chocolate

Chocolate tastes like,
Sweet flour
And a cold glass of white milk.

Chocolate smells like,
Heaven so sweet.
When I just think,
It is just a treat.

Chocolate feels like,
Cream and biscuits
Mixed together.

Chocolate looks like
A big cubed brown bar
That is melty.

Chocolate sounds like
Crunching leaves
On the floor during autumn.

Dara Akinola (6)
King's House Preparatory School & Nursery, Luton

My Favourite Snack

They smell yummy like little bits of chips.
I like the salt and vinegar type, they taste delicious if I take a bite.
They look spiky like a dinosaur's spine.
I like the sound of a packet of crisps opening, it's like fireworks at night.
They feel like salt on my hands.

Barack Nyamboki (7)
King's House Preparatory School & Nursery, Luton

All About Arya

She smells of freshly washed clothes
And fruity shampoo
The scent of fresh-cut grass when we
go outside to play
Makes her smell as lovely as a summer's day
That's my sister, Arya.

She is as loud and cheery
As a crazy kangaroo
When we play hide-and-seek
She laughs ecstatically and shouts 'boo'!

We both love tasting ripe, juicy grapes
Tangy, spicy chicken and
Delicious, yummy cakes!

I love stroking her silky, soft hair
I always hold her tiny, little hands
As we walk together
And climb each stair.

I love looking at the world through
Her gorgeous green eyes
I hate to see her sweet face upset
When she cries
I will always protect her
And never let her come to any harm
We will always be together arm in arm.

That's my sister Arya!

Aleena Azam (7)
King's House Preparatory School & Nursery, Luton

My Mum!

My mum smells like sweet perfume.
She always asks me why and never just assumes.

She looks like the Quen.
She is always kind and never mean.

She feels like berries as squashy as a banana,
And says my dad should have been a farmer!

She sounds like a happy bird chirping all day.
When I finish my homework she lets me play.

She tastes as sweet as a cherry.
I love my mum as she is always very merry!

Amber-Zahra Abbas (6)
King's House Preparatory School & Nursery, Luton

Summer

In the summer, it is beautiful green, bright and sunny.
Plants grow quicker.
Grass gets greener.
Fruits get sweeter.
Feel the hot sun on my skin.
Listen to the birds singing.
Smell the lovely fragrance of the beautiful flowers.
Oh how I love summer!

Stephanie Oghenemine Ogban (7)
King's House Preparatory School & Nursery, Luton

Dancing

Hey! Haven't you seen and heard
How I like to twirl and soar in the sky like a bird?
It makes me feel like an ugly duckling
turning into a swan.
It's like sucking your favourite sweet and having that taste linger on your tongue.
Listen to the vibrations bouncing off the wall
and the floor.
Look at the amazing moves I can do, if you watch carefully you can do them too.
Dancing entices you with its scent of an aromatic rose that has just bloomed.

Imaan Shahieen Khan (6)
King's House Preparatory School & Nursery, Luton

Plums And Peaches

My favourite fruits are plums and peaches
They grow on trees with lots of branches
They are lovely and sweet, just the perfect treat!
They look delicious and are very nutritious!
Plums are shiny and smooth
But I still prefer peaches to tell you the truth.
Plums and peaches smell like flowers
After eating them I get special powers!

Haaris Javaid (7)
King's House Preparatory School & Nursery, Luton

Fruit

Melon is my favourite fruit
But it's not really sour.
Lemons are strong
Because they give you lots of power.

Strawberries are red
And full of vitamin C.
When you need a boost
Strawberries are key!

Apples are juicy
And also very crunchy.
They are a perfect snack
For when you get the munchies.

Bananas are yellow
Also very long.
One banana a day
Keeps you fit and strong.

Joaquim Bangaroo (7)
King's House Preparatory School & Nursery, Luton

Crisps

Heaven so salty, melting in my mouth, feels like some dancing in my hands.
It smells like salt, and it also sounds like
flowers growing.
Looks like shining paper.

Kristal Dongbakuro (6)
King's House Preparatory School & Nursery, Luton

My Family

I like my family. They like me.
I like to hold my baby brother and kiss my family.
I like when I can smell my dad's hair gel.
Christian music makes me think about my family and my dad playing the guitar.
When I can smell chicken it makes me
think about my family.
Seeing my grandma and grandad makes me think how lucky I am to have a family like I do.
When I see pictures of my family, I like to go to them and say, 'I love you!'

Nahum Joshua Alexis Abiaka (7)
King's House Preparatory School & Nursery, Luton

The Rabbit

I hear rabbits hopping along
The rabbit's name is Fluffy.
Fluffy he is to touch
Oh how I like to stroke him so much!

I see Fluffy Rabbit hopping along
He loves the taste of cheese
When I smell him he makes me sneeze.

He is my friend.

Maya Brown (6)
King's House Preparatory School & Nursery, Luton

My Toothbrush

My toothbrush is
black and green.
The bristles smell
fresh and clean.
I have mint toothpaste
which Mummy tells me never to waste.
The handle is made of
rubber and plastic.
I can grip it hard
it's fantastic!
When I turn it on
it vibrates.
As I brush and scrub
my hand shakes.
Morning and night
my teeth are squeaking.
When I smile
they look sparkling!

Sheharyar Butt (6)
King's House Preparatory School & Nursery, Luton

Inspire Swimming Pool

I arrive at the swimming pool for my lesson
inside I see the children having fun
I hear teachers shouting, children laughing
and parents saying, 'Well done son.'

I get changed and climb into the pool
it feels warm on my skin
I put my head above the water
I feel a draught on my chin.

I start to swim across the swimming pool
but some water gets in my mouth
It tastes disgusting like slimy seaweed
or like the toothpaste in my house.

I get out and have a shower
it smells like a soapy drain
I put my wet clothes in my bag
they smell of the autumn forest rain!

Ryyan Akhtar (6)
King's House Preparatory School & Nursery, Luton

My Chocolate Poem

Chocolate sounds like leaves crunching in autumn.
When you eat a chocolate it goes to your tummy.
Chocolate tastes sweet like sugar.
I could eat it on an aeroplane.
Chocolate feels smooth like silk.
Chocolate is made out of milk.
Some chocolates look like a bouncy ball.
Chocolates look big and small.
Chocolate smells very minty.

Amaana Rahman (6)
King's House Preparatory School & Nursery, Luton

Cars

The moon is shining as I stand and listen.
I hear the loud roaring sounds of big chunking tyres.
As it comes around the corner I
can't believe what I see.
A long, black, amazing car moving like a panther through the night.
It stops.
I move forward.
It feels like a smooth, silky blanket, I think.
What would it taste like?
It would be hard to bite and taste like nasty Chinese!
I open the door and sit inside.
I take a deep breath.
It smells like strawberry bubblegum
And the seats feel as smooth as fur.

Taan Sangha (7)
King's House Preparatory School & Nursery, Luton

My Little Brother

I saw my brother crawling
Moving forward and falling.
He tries to touch and grab everything
I help him when he starts struggling.
It makes me sad and angry
When I hear him crying.
He smells his food before eating
And says, 'No,' sometimes before starting.
He doesn't like the taste of baby food
Curry is the one food I have found him enjoying!

Umar Mazhar (6)
King's House Preparatory School & Nursery, Luton

My Sense Poem

We can see the stars.
If we hear it I have to dance to the music.
You can smell the washing machine.
You can show your Chinese food when you want to.

Adedamola Adeoti (5)
King's House Preparatory School & Nursery, Luton

Summer

Summer feels like a hot cross bun,
like a baked cake in an oven.
Summer smells like a barbecue party,
Umm! It can get very sticky and sweaty.
Summer tastes like a warm dream,
Such fun to have a melting ice cream.
Summer sounds like a day off from school,
Enjoy a splash at the swimming pool.
Summer days are nice and bright,
You can see a lot of sunlight.

Aansh Lohia (5)
King's House Preparatory School & Nursery, Luton

Cricket Poem

I like to play cricket
When I'm batting I won't hit the wicket
I like to smell the fresh air
It always blows through my hair
I always look at the hard ball
And I hit it over the wall.

Aayan Chowdhry (6)
King's House Preparatory School & Nursery, Luton

Silly Socks

Silly socks smell like skunks.
Silly socks look like they need to go in the washing machine.
Silly socks sound like snacks breaking.
Silly socks taste like something disgusting.

Eugene London Jordan (6)
King's House Preparatory School & Nursery, Luton

My Spaghetti And Meatballs Poem

Spaghetti and meatballs sound tinkly when I put them on the fork.
Spaghetti and meatballs smell like fresh tomato sauce in my nose.
Spaghetti and meatballs taste sweet and salty like mixed popcorn.
Spaghetti and meatballs feel very chewy and slimy
and soft.
Spaghetti and meatballs look like brown balls and white wiggly worms!

Ayesha Raza (6)
King's House Preparatory School & Nursery, Luton

Oranges

Oranges taste so sweet and nice.
Their smell teases your appetite.
If you take and squeeze them you can make yummy juice.
When kids see and hear them they put smiles and happiness in their eyes,
pouring,
can't wait to jump off the school bus.

Juliette Mitrov (6)
King's House Preparatory School & Nursery, Luton

Disneyland

Disneyland fireworks sound fantastic and sometimes scary.
Disneyland ice cream and candyfloss taste so sweet and yummy.
Disneyland Princess Elsa and Anna feel so lovely to touch and Mickey mouse feels so huggly.
Disneyland castle looks so bright like sunshine.

Disneyland trains produce so much smoke which smells like paper burning.

Kayla Choto (6)
King's House Preparatory School & Nursery, Luton

Ice Cream

Ice cream you taste of bubblegum.
Ice cream you smell like the freezing-cold wind.
Ice cream you look like all the different colours in the rainbow.
Ice cream you feel smooth like a fluffy cloud.
Ice cream you sound silent!

Leeya Naik Ehsan (5)
King's House Preparatory School & Nursery, Luton

Mum's Cooking

Mum's cooking smells delicious.
It comes in different shapes and sizes.
Mum's cooking is very colourful.
Green is for vegctable; red, orange, yellow
are for fruits.
Mum's cooking makes a bubbling and sizzling sound.
Crispy onion and tofu are my favourite foods.
Mum's cooking tastes wonderful.
Sweet and sour is the number one choice.
Mum's cooking feels warm and lovely.
Mum's cooking is the best in the world.

Megan Yu (5)
King's House Preparatory School & Nursery, Luton

Great Barrier Reef

All the wonderful sea creatures are beneath the blue ocean.
The freezing-cold water that runs in a
smoothing motion.
The smell of fresh air that makes us want to care.
Tasting the salty water and seeing a jellyfish
with her daughter.

Riley Emerton (6)
King's House Preparatory School & Nursery, Luton

Ice Cream

Ice cream smells like fresh sea breeze
When it's creamy it tastes very good.
Ice cream looks like fresh-made yoghurt
But really it looks like vanilla or chocolate.
Ice cream tastes like frosty mornings and cold days
With an icy-cold drink on a hot summer's day!
Ice cream feels as cold as lemonade
And as cold as Antarctica can be.
Ice cream sounds like smooth music when it melts
And sounds as soft as a rabbit bouncing.

Joy Hayble (7)
King's House Preparatory School & Nursery, Luton

Untitled

Chocolate looks brown.
Chocolate tastes like milk, cold from the fridge,
and it's mine.
Chocolate crunches when you eat it.

Ethan Igali (5)
Our Lady's Catholic Primary School, Stockport

Untitled

Chocolate is brown.
Chocolate tastes yummy.
Chocolate feels soft.
Chocolate smells delicious.
Chocolate makes a cracking sound.

Brihanna Sandra Estevao Manuel (4)
Our Lady's Catholic Primary School, Stockport

Untitled

Chocolate is delicious.
Chocolate is yellow.
Chocolate tastes like milk.
Chocolate feels cold.
Chocolate makes a cracking sound.
I love chocolate.

Lexi Cooper-Jones (5)
Our Lady's Catholic Primary School, Stockport

Untitled

Chocolate is brown.
Chocolate tastes good.
Chocolate feels hard.
Chocolate smells minty.
Chocolate makes a cracking sound.

Kyle James Barlow (5)
Our Lady's Catholic Primary School, Stockport

Chocolate Fun For Everyone

Chocolate is gooey.
Chocolate is hard.
Chocolate is milky.
Chocolate is browny and white.
Chocolate makes a crack.

Annalese Wood (5)
Our Lady's Catholic Primary School, Stockport

Chocolate

Chocolate is sweet.
Chocolate is milk.
Chocolate makes a crack.
Chocolate is smooth.
Chocolate is brown.

Owen Tierney (4)
Our Lady's Catholic Primary School, Stockport

My Milkshake Poem

Milkshake, milkshake feels like silk.
Milkshake, milkshake is made out of milk.
Milkshake, milkshake tastes so sweet.
Milkshake, milkshake, it's just like a big treat.
Milkshake, milkshake is so yummy.
Milkshake, milkshake, I wish I can drink it in my tummy.

Safa Qasim (7)
Paradise Primary School, Dewsbury

Super Sour Sweets

Sweets taste really yummy
Sweets taste as sweet as a dummy
Sweets are really yummy
They smell like delicious dummies
They smell yummy, just smell sweets
I hear the sweets crumbling
It always sounds wonderful
Sweets feel sticky but they actually feel lovely!

Sara Hazi (7)
Paradise Primary School, Dewsbury

Lovely Fruits

I wake up early in the morning, what do I see?
A yummy, yummy cherry!
It looks like a berry
It tastes like a strawberry
I hear it, it is very juicy!
My hands now smell all fruity
Eating them all, I feel happy!

Aisha Bodhania (5)
Paradise Primary School, Dewsbury

Grapes Grapes

Grapes, grapes
Grapes, grapes taste like sweets,
Grapes, grapes, I can eat them in the streets
Grapes, grapes smell like ice,
Grapes, grapes are so yummy and nice,
Grapes, grapes are shiny green,
Grapes, grapes are very juicy and clean,
Grapes, grapes look like treats,
If I don't get any I will scream!

Yusuf Dokrat (8)
Paradise Primary School, Dewsbury

Spring

Spring tastes like a cookie with icing.
Spring looks like a beautiful season.
Spring smells like fresh flowers.
Spring feels like a fluffy bunny.
Spring sounds like a bird tweeting.

Khadija Abdelkadir (6)
Paradise Primary School, Dewsbury

One Beautiful Morning

I woke up in the
Morning, I looked
Out the window
I saw the yellow
Sun smiling.
I opened the door
And smelt the roses
Then I went in
And touched
My cup of tea to see if it had
Cooled down.
I tasted my tea
And it was nice and warm.
Today was going to be a nice day.

Humayra Patel (6)
Paradise Primary School, Dewsbury

Chocolate – My Favourite Snack

It's yummy, dark chocolate,
Very smooth like a big, flat booklet,
Delicious chocolates that I can touch,
I can have them all day, I like it very much,
Yummy chocolate, it's very rare,
It's like a smooth, thin piece of hair.

Khadija Ibrahim (7)
Paradise Primary School, Dewsbury

Sweet Ice Cream

Chocolate ice cream
Strawberry ice cream
Tastes like a dream
When I touch it my fingers freeze

Ice cream van
Ice cream van
I can hear you sing
I'm going to buy everything

Everybody come and see
It's time to smell a delicious, sweet treat!

Eesa Khan (6)
Paradise Primary School, Dewsbury

My Lemon

Lemon, Lemon, you taste sweet.
Lemon, Lemon, you smell nice.
Lemon, Lemon, when I touch you, you are so smooth.
Lemon, Lemon, I can hear you squeak.
Lemon, Lemon, I can see you in the fridge.

Maryam Bint Tariq (8)
Paradise Primary School, Dewsbury

Saudi Arabia

I can hear the birds' beautiful tweets
With their big golden beaks
I can touch the sun
It feels like a bun,
I'm bursting with a beam
It's not a dream
I'm having a juicy date
With my friendly mate
I can see the birds
With a lot of words
There they go
First they leap
Before you or I could say
They will do it
They're so deep
The smell is the best
perfume.

Aishah Noor Naeem (7)
Paradise Primary School, Dewsbury

Lamborghini

Lamborghini, it rides like the storm, it is a lovely Lamborghini
It feels like a golden engine, it has super speed, it looks like golden coins
Lamborghini, when it drives like a storm it comes out with smoke
I hear a fast engine, it's like a cheetah running, it is as fast as a storm, a storm with lightning
If you ride it you'll like it, it has super speed
I've never had one but I would buy it if I was rich!

Abdur-Rahman Obeidi (7)
Paradise Primary School, Dewsbury

My Favourite Thing

I can see the rainbow in my dreams
I can imagine it while I am doing anything
I can hear the wind blowing
In my dreams I can hear the wind blowing the rainbow from one place to another
I can imagine me in my mind touching the rainbow
The smell of the rainbow is just like shine
The taste of the rainbow is like the rainbow shining brightly in the daytime.

Fatima Zahra Patel (8)
Paradise Primary School, Dewsbury

My Favourite Chocolate

I can taste the white chocolate which is like white rice,
I can hear the bumpy chocolate which is like a
white cat miaowing,
I can touch the delicious chocolate which is like
a bumpy hill,
I can see the chocolate which is as white as
the school rabbit,
I can smell the chocolate which smells really nice,
Chocolate, chocolate tastes so nice!

Habeebah Raja (7)
Paradise Primary School, Dewsbury

Milkshakes

Milkshakes are nice
They feel like cold ice
Ooh... they are so nice
They taste like cream
If I don't have it I may scream.

Abu-Bakr Polli (8)
Paradise Primary School, Dewsbury

My Toy Kitten

My toy kitten, Alveira
My toy kitten, Alveira
Whenever I see her lying around, she shows me a lovely smile

I always hear her purr and miaow,
Isn't it a lovely sound?

She smells so nice like strong-smelling perfume,
And somehow she spreads it all around me.

It's so sad that one day she got lost,
I hope that a hungry dog didn't eat her and think she tasted delicious.

Oh my little kitten, she's so soft,
I once imagined she was a fluffy, round cotton ball.

Eesha Ismail (7)
Paradise Primary School, Dewsbury

Spider-Man

Spider-Man smells salty.
Spider-Man looks like a superhero.
Spider-Man sounds like whispering.
Spider-Man feels like webs.
Spider-Man tastes like spiders.

Aidan Kidd (6)
Petteril Bank Community School, Carlisle

Smarties

Smarties sound like a baby's rattle.
Smarties taste like creamy chocolate.
Smarties smell nice, like hot chocolate.
Smarties look like the colours of the rainbow.
Smarties feel smooth like a pebble.

Reuben Massey (5)
Rosley CE School, Wigton

Cat

Cats look like black and white fur.
Cats smell like mice and rats.
Cats taste like fish and mice.
Cats sound like moaning.
Cats feel like the fluff of a lumpy cloud.

Thea Reid (6)
Rosley CE School, Wigton

Sharks

The slap of a shark's tail sounds like
the bang of a drum.
They taste as salty as the sea.
They feel like a slippery snake.
They look as big as an Indian elephant.
They smell as fishy as a seal or a penguin.

Oscar Massey (7)
Rosley CE School, Wigton

My House

My house sounds like doors banging.
My house feels rough like cement.
My house looks like hard rocks.
My house smells like perfume.
My house tastes like hot sausages.

Jack Turner (5)
Rosley CE School, Wigton

Holidays

Holidays sound like laughter and fun.
Holidays feel like white sand going through my fingers.
Holidays taste like lovely ice cream.
Holidays smell like salty sea rocking against the shore.
Holidays look like sandy beaches.

Rosemary Elizabeth Quinn (5)
Rosley CE School, Wigton

A Bag Of Crisps

Crisps sound like going *snap!*
Crisps taste like sea salt.
Crisps feel bumpy and spiky, like a hedgehog.
Crisps look like slices of sweet potato.
Crisps smell like salt and vinegar or prawn cocktail.

Kara Eve Thomlinson (7)
Rosley CE School, Wigton

Usain Bolt

He sees crowds when he goes to races.
He tastes like salty seaweed.
He smells like sweat.
He feels like drops of water.
He sounds like thunderbolts.

Daniel Patrick Keane (6)
Rosley CE School, Wigton

A Strawberry

When I am eating a strawberry, it sounds like squishy juice.
It tastes like juice and pips mixed together.
It smells like summer fruits.
It looks like a red ball of blood.
It feels like squishy cream.

Felix Broadbent (6)
Rosley CE School, Wigton

Cheese

Cheese tastes like sour milk.
Cheese can feel hard or soft.
Cheese smells like flour and milk.
Cheese looks yellow-gold.
Cheese sounds squeaky.

Bella Milburn (6)
Rosley CE School, Wigton

Spain

Spain feels like the sand between your toes.
Spain looks beautiful.
Spain smells like summer.
Spain would taste like sun – not quite!
Spain sounds like Heaven!

Hope Vernon (5)
Rosley CE School, Wigton

Dinosaur

Dinosaurs sound like a giant's roar.
Dinosaurs feel like scales.
Dinosaurs look red and black.
Dinosaurs smell like blood.
Dinosaurs taste yucky.

Finley Graham (6)
Rosley CE School, Wigton

Pancakes

Pancakes taste like eggs and milk and flour.
Pancakes look like 2D circles.
Pancakes smell like milk and golden syrup.
Pancakes feel like omelettes.
Pancakes sound like bacon sizzling in a pan.

Sam Donald (7)
Rosley CE School, Wigton

A Snake

A snake sounds like this – *sss!*
A snake feels like a sea creature.
A snake tastes like rotten eggs.
A snake smells like sweet grass.
A snake looks camouflaged in the long, green grass.

Isaac Joe Rumney (5)
Rosley CE School, Wigton

Mum's House

My mum's house smells like chips.
My mum's house tastes like chocolate.
My mum's house sounds like clocks ticking.
My mum's house feels rocky like stones.
My mum's house looks like a bungalow.

Charlie Robert Jackson (5)
Rosley CE School, Wigton

A Holiday

A holiday sounds like the waves crashing in the sea.
A holiday feels like the sand on your feet.
A holiday looks like a beautiful garden.
A holiday smells like the fresh air.
A holiday tastes like burgers and ice cream.

Lily Mary Richardson (6)
Rosley CE School, Wigton

Chocolate

Chocolate tastes like Heaven.
Chocolate makes a crack like a twig when you eat it.
Chocolate feels like a smooth pebble.
Chocolate smells like scrummy Smarties.
Chocolate looks like a brown tree.

Rory Irving (6)
Rosley CE School, Wigton

Crisps

Crisp bags go *pop* when I open the bag.
Crisps taste like sea salt.
Crisps smell as strong as the sea.
Crisps look big and yellow, like the sun.
Crisps feel like a bumpy or smooth surface.

Hannah Emily Kelly (7)
Rosley CE School, Wigton

Cheese

Cheese sounds like clattering when you chop it.
Cheese feels cold when you get it out of the fridge.
Cheese looks more yellow than the sun.
Cheese smells like milk and eggs.
Cheese tastes like yellow squares.

Lucy Knott (6)
Rosley CE School, Wigton

London's Burning!

Rush! Rush! Out of the door.
Fire! Fire! All around my house.
I can see the fire eating our city.
My eyes are orange, my house is yellow,
my face is red.
I hope I find a safe place for my children and me.
I am scared of going out. Can you come with me?
I can hear cracking fire in the air.
People are shouting and screaming near my house.

Halle Miller (7)
Tarporley CE Primary School, Tarporley

London's Burning Town

I can see lots of people screaming.
I can hear the houses falling down.
I can smell the wood of the houses.
I can feel lots of thick smoke.

Samuel M Preston (6)
Tarporley CE Primary School, Tarporley

Fire Through The Door

Orange flames, quickly spreading around my house.
Rush, rush, through the door.
Red and orange flames went through my door.
All around my house were crackling flames.
Trapped in the kitchen, everything was in flames.
I wasn't scared but it was spreading.
That's all I could see, red zooming flames, all around the city and my house.
Everything was red.

Nathan Anderton (7)
Tarporley CE Primary School, Tarporley

London Sparks

Hearing your wife yelling, 'There is a flaming fire!'
Pulling and grabbing me out of bed quickly, so I can get out of the thick, black, grey smoke.
Red, hot, flaming fire, coming in faster and faster!
Grey, smelly smoke coming in faster and faster and hearing people yelling.
Thick, burning, black smoke, coming in the house, everybody yelling.
Crackling, burning fire on the roof.

Leah Cunningham (7)
Tarporley CE Primary School, Tarporley

London's Great Fire

Dashing and running, out of the house!
Fire! Fire! All around the city.
In can see dashing flames burning the roofs of
houses and churches.
Look out of the window! People are getting burned. What shall we do?
I can smell crackling wood burning the floor.
I can feel fire burning rotten walls.
I can taste smoky air going down my throat.

Harry Leftwick (7)
Tarporley CE Primary School, Tarporley

London's Sparks!

What's that light? It should be night!
Dash! Run! Out of the door, the fire is coming
up our floor.
I can see crackly flames, filling the misty, mucky sky.
I can smell smoke everywhere so we can't see.
Run! Away from the rats. If they bite you,
you will be poisoned forever.
People splashing around in the River Thames.
Fire rapidly and furiously eating all the houses.
Horrified people running for their lives.
Oh no! People are getting burned!
What should we do?

Milly Venning (7)
Tarporley CE Primary School, Tarporley

Fly In The Sky

Fly! Fly! In the sky,
See little bees flying by.
Taste sweet nectar and hear fluttering wings,
Pollen tickling my nose (I could now just sneeze).
I can see tiny dots of people and a sea of poppies, swaying in the wind, like a bright red ocean.
Smelling, perfumed flowers and a sound of birds singing softly to me.
Collecting fresh food for my tea.
The sweet whistle of summer breeze
creeping up on me.
I can see soft, velvety petals.

Holly Slaughter (7)
Tarporley CE Primary School, Tarporley

London's Sparks

Rush! Rush! Out of the door.
Fire! Fire! It's everywhere!
Oh no! It's spreading!

I hear the crackling sound of flaming fire,
People screaming like a snake.
They shout, 'Escape! Escape!'
It's chaos. It goes on and on.

I see yellow and red flames going up,
Raging fire on top of the tumbled-down houses.
Yeah! The rats are dead!

Rebecca Line (7)
Tarporley CE Primary School, Tarporley

In My Bed, What's That I Can Smell?

Smoke, quickly coming from my door.
I looked in the window. It was so bright, with light all over the place.

'Help! Help! London's burning!' Everyone shouting like a tiger roaring.
The fire spreading quickly.
Rush! Rush! Quickly!
Get out of the door quick!
The fire was heading to the west.
There was a man called Samuel Pepys and he said,
'If this bright light is spreading down the streets, pull the houses down.'
So they pulled the houses down.
There were flames everywhere.

George Wood (6)
Tarporley CE Primary School, Tarporley

London's Flaming Fire

I was chasing out of the house because loads of flaming fire was chasing me.
I smell wooden, hot houses, getting killed by the
big, gigantic fire.
I could hear crackling, creepy, scratchy fire.
Rush! Rush! What's that light?
Something was burning me. I was tucked under my red, cosy cover.
I ran to the burning, hot door.
I could hear people screaming in the city!

Marcus Kearney (6)
Tarporley CE Primary School, Tarporley

The Great Fire Of London

I can hear crackling flames nearby and people shouting at me.
I see big, orange, red and yellow fire outside my
little, wooden cottage.
Quickly! It's near!
I need to escape from the smoky air.
I can feel the hot, flaming fire and it's getting closer.
In my mouth, I can taste the ashy, smoky flames.
I am trying to put the fire out with the
heavy leather buckets.

Ella Jones (6)
Tarporley CE Primary School, Tarporley

London Burning

Dash, dash out of the wooden door, fire all around
my home.
I can smell sickly, smoky air, filling my nostrils.
I can smell rotting wood.
I can hear crackling flames, eating my city.
I can hear people screaming for help.
I can feel the warmth of ashy air.
I can see fire rapidly spreading, the flames furiously wrecking my city.

Jared Mills (7)
Tarporley CE Primary School, Tarporley

The Crackling Fire Of London

I can see flaming fire, eating my city quickly.
I can feel hot flames nearby.
I can hear crackling fire.
I can taste smoke in the air.
I can smell burning wood in the air.

Aidan Hart (7)
Tarporley CE Primary School, Tarporley

The Crackling Fire Of London

Dash! Dash! Out of the door.
Fire's spreading all over my city.

I can see fire, crackling on houses.
I can hear crackling flames and people screaming.
I can feel my daddy's hand because I am scared.
I can smell smoke.
I can see fire rapidly spreading.
My eyes are blinded because of the fire.
I can see sparks and wood burning.
I am starting to get hot because fire is hot.
I can see flaming fire.

Helen Riley (6)
Tarporley CE Primary School, Tarporley

The Big Burn

Dash! Dash ! Out of the house!
I can smell the crackling flames, rapidly spreading across the dusty streets.
I can smell the rotting wood,
spreading around the city.
A shy air running around the city of London.
I can hear the crackling flames all over the door
and everywhere.
Red flames, dashing back and forth, through the city.

Jack Farren (6)
Tarporley CE Primary School, Tarporley

London's Flaming Fire

Dash! Dash! Out of the door.
Fire! Fire! It's going everywhere.
Through the windows, I can see
horrified people dashing.
I can hear crackling flames from the fire.
The fire is quickly coming to my lane!
I can feel the burning smoke on my cheeks.
As I run down the River Thames, I can taste the flaming, smoky air.

Luke O'Hara Clarke (7)
Tarporley CE Primary School, Tarporley

The Great Fire!

Rush! Rush! Out of the door.
Fire! Fire! All around my home.
Flame filling my world,
The flames on each and every home.
Yellow flames licking the sky.
I could feel the fiery wood on my hands,
The fire eating everything.

Rhys Chambers (7)
Tarporley CE Primary School, Tarporley

London Burning

Rush! Run out of the door.
Fire! Fire! My house is on fire!
It is eating my city.
I can see the fire spreading quickly cross the streets.
I can smell the flames and smoke in the air.
I can taste burning in my mouth.
I can feel the smoke on my face.
I hope the fire burns down soon.

Gemma Randles (6)
Tarporley CE Primary School, Tarporley

London Sparks

Rush! Rush! Out of the door.
I can smell the fire under my floor.
I can see orange, yellow fire, like bombs flashing in my eyes, in the dark mist.
I can taste the fire, going left and right, high and low.
People shouting, 'Go! Go! Go!'
I can hear crackling flames, going left and right.

Isobelle Allan (6)
Tarporley CE Primary School, Tarporley

Clear Ice

Fresh water
Cool and wet
Smell of fresh air
Pitter-patter.

Katie Emma Jordan (6)
Towerview Primary School, Bangor

Countryside!

Countryside! Countryside! So many things to see!
Birds swooping, trees swaying, rivers rushing by.
As I touch the trees, the bark feels rough to the skin.
The holly hurts when I touch it!
I can taste the ferns and the fresh air.
I can smell the river air.
I can hear the birds singing sweetly.
I can hear the leaves rustle and the splashing river.

Ethan Greenaway (7)
Upton Cross Primary School, Liskeard

Me And My Teddy

I hear my teddy singing a song to send me to sleep.
I can feel my teddy all night because I
cuddle my teddy all night.
I can see darkness in the night.
I can smell hot chocolate and strawberries.

Issy Thom (7)
Upton Cross Primary School, Liskeard

Miss Batten

Her voice sounds happy.
Her skin is soft.
She looks like a nice girl.
She smells like perfume.
I don't know what she tastes like!

Naomi Bettison (7)
Upton Cross Primary School, Liskeard

The Martial Arts

I can hear my mates shouting!
I can taste my creamy Milky Way when we get a break.
I can smell my mate's sweat!
I can see my instructor showing me what to do.
I can touch the pad when I kick super powerfully!

Bobby Easton Evans (7)
Upton Cross Primary School, Liskeard

Gymnastics

I hear the bounce when I bounce on a trampoline.
I taste the breeze when I sprint.
I smell other people.
I see that I am bouncing high.
I swing on the bars and it's so much fun.

Lauren Hoare (7)
Upton Cross Primary School, Liskeard

My Dog

I can feel the fluff on my dog's soft body.
It feels very soft.
I can see my brown, fluffy dog's bone.
I can smell super special air.
I can hear my dog barking.

Poppy Amelia Carthew-Hall (6)
Upton Cross Primary School, Liskeard

Lego

I can hear clicking.
I can smell nothing.
I can taste dirt.
I can see bright and colourful Lego.
I can feel hard pieces of Lego.

Caine Hosband (7)
Upton Cross Primary School, Liskeard

The Beach

I can hear seagulls squawking.
I can touch sand, as smooth as Play-Doh.
I can see sand, and water as blue as sky.
I can smell ice cream.
I can taste sandwiches.

Holly Stock (7)
Upton Cross Primary School, Liskeard

Me And Hope

When I ride my pony, I can hear hooves
clipping and clopping.
I can feel the rough reins.
I can smell a sweet and musty smell.
I can taste delicious horse food.

Holly Merriner (7)
Upton Cross Primary School, Liskeard

Today I Ate A Worm

Today I ate a worm.
It tasted horrible.
It felt like jelly,
So I spat it out!

Warren Banks (5)
Well Lane Primary School, Birkenhead

Worms

Today I ate a worm.
It tasted yucky.
It felt slimy.
It danced in my mouth,
So I spat it out!

Sophia Kaplansoy (5)
Well Lane Primary School, Birkenhead

Pancakes

Pancakes sound like bubbles in a bath.
Pancakes taste like Smarties.
Pancakes feel like a soft pillow.
Pancakes smell like bananas.
Pancakes look like birds.

Leah Sysum (6)
Well Lane Primary School, Birkenhead

Pancakes

Pancakes smell like Heaven.
Pancakes sound like bubbles.
Pancakes taste like life.
Pancakes feel like pillows.
Pancakes look like a Frisbee.

Michael Kinealy (7)
Well Lane Primary School, Birkenhead

Pancakes

Pancakes look like a burger.
Pancakes smell like my lovely home.
Pancakes taste like sweet candy.
Pancakes feel like the soft, good snow.
Pancakes sound like a jingle in the sky.

Max Hibbert (6)
Well Lane Primary School, Birkenhead

Untitled

Pancakes smell like syrup.
Pancakes taste like sugar.
Pancakes look like an apple.
Pancakes sound like popping circles.
Pancakes feel crispy.

Maddison Amis (6)
Well Lane Primary School, Birkenhead

Pancakes

Pancakes smell like bananas.
Pancakes look like bears.
Pancakes taste like sugar.
Pancakes feel like a teddy.
Pancakes sound like people.

Caitlyn Louise Wellman (7)
Well Lane Primary School, Birkenhead

Pancakes

Pancakes smell like sugar.
Pancakes taste like strawberries.
Pancakes sound like zzz.
Pancakes feel soft.
Pancakes look like a soft pillow.

Lola Makay (7)
Well Lane Primary School, Birkenhead

Untitled

Pancakes smell like bananas.
Pancakes sound like burgers in a pan.
Pancakes taste like sugar.
Pancakes feel like the soft pillow.
Pancakes look like the sun.

Fletcher Hagan (7)
Well Lane Primary School, Birkenhead

Young Writers Information

We hope you have enjoyed reading this book and that you will continue to in the coming years.

If you're a young writer who enjoys reading and creative writing, or the parent of an enthusiastic poet or story writer, do visit our website **www.youngwriters.co.uk**. Here you will find free competitions, workshops and games, as well as recommended reads, a poetry glossary and our blog.

If you would like to order further copies of this book, or any of our other titles give us a call or visit **www.youngwriters.co.uk**.

Young Writers
Remus House
Coltsfoot Drive
Peterborough
PE2 9BF

(01733) 890066
info@youngwriters.co.uk

Share your feelings verse any time!